To Cary & Mary

Good Luck!

Bunny

MY NIGHT

BARRY GRAY

PEOPLE

SIMON AND SCHUSTER / NEW YORK

Library of Congress Cataloging in Publication Data

Gray, Barry.
    Barry Gray: My night people.

    Autobiographical.
    1.   Gray, Barry, 1916–   I.   Title.
PN1991.4.G69A35   070.4'3'0924 [B]   75–14039
ISBN 0–671–22090–X

To Manuis and Dora Yaroslaw, my father and mother. Who gave me life. And hope.

It started when a guy named Steve Ellis was getting laid. He hosted an all-night radio program on WOR, then the flagship station of the Mutual network. He was short, heavy, barrel-chested, ruggedly good-looking, with the charming smile of a con man, and he had a club foot. That foot seemed to work its fetish attraction on lots of women. Steve played it big, too. He wanted to "know" all those women, biblically, before he died. And on balance, he damn near made it.

His program was called *Moonlight Saving Time*, and it went on the air each morning at 2, and ended at 5:45. It was aimed at the musical tastes of restaurant countermen, factory hands, and Rosie the Riveter, for it was World War II, and it had been concocted as a broadcast backdrop to the work of busy hands and minds, fashioning war machinery. Steve made $175 per week, and he played albums of fifteen minutes' duration throughout the night, which gave him ample opportunity for his chosen avocation, the study of the female form, in other, vacant studios of the deserted broadcast shop just off Times Square. Talent for Steve was easily available. The hub of New York crawled with ready volunteers. They were, in the main, known as "V" girls, for they "made it" chiefly with servicemen—hoping, I guess, to screw the Allies to victory.

I had arrived in New York within that year, just out of

the Army and with some radio experience prior to the service years, and walked into WOR to nose around. I was still in uniform, having taken advantage of the furlough rates of the railroads for servicemen in those years, which enabled me to ride the day coach from the West Coast to New York for about $40. The chief announcer auditioned me and hired me, and that afternoon, still wearing OD's, I was doing staff announcing work and meeting people like Leon Janney, who was then "Chick Carter, Boy Detective."

After a break-in period I was assigned to "remotes"— that is, going to the various night spots which then abounded in New York. There I'd announce quarter-hour and half-hour broadcasts of music performed by Louis Prima at the Astor or Sammy Kaye or Xavier Cugat at the Waldorf, Al Trace at the Dixie, Vaughn Monroe at the Commodore, and in short, shag my ass off, running from one remote to another from 6 in the evening until 2 A.M., with fifteen-minute, or perhaps half-hour, transit breaks to get from one place to another. The pay: $59 a week, plus transportation. I walked, but I put in for cab fares, for which I was reimbursed weekly, and without that swindle of $6 or $8 a week my life-style would have suffered death.

At the time, it was considered the best staff job in radio, and if you were lucky enough to be in the best hotels, awaiting their broadcast at dinnertime, the food was on the house. Unfortunately, I usually found myself in dumps. Senior men drew the Waldorf, Roosevelt, Astor, etcetera—that is, at dinnertime. For many of the places did two broadcasts nightly, one for the East Coast and another, hours later, for the West Coast, allowing for the three-hour time differential. The new men, like me, drew the late shows: therefore, no dinner.

At 2 in the morning the network schedule ceased, and more than 400 Mutual stations around the country took over their local programming. And those of us doing remotes would report back to the studio to file our logs (affidavits of performance, time on the air, off the air, irregularities, etcetera) and generally repair to a place called Toffenetti's, just across from the old Paramount Theater, on the site now occupied by Nathan's. The food was cheap, and it was cheap. It wasn't good and cheap. Steve Ellis would now be on the air with his saccharine "Good morning, folks. This is *Moonlight Saving Time*— your musical favorites throughout the night, until five forty-five . . ." and he then clump-clumped down the hall with his "bride" of the night for his score.

One night the turntable got stuck, or a member of management called, or the engineer had to leave for the urinal. At any rate, someone ratted on Steve. He confessed—no, he bragged. He was fired. And on the way out, he turned and spoke immortal words: "Oh, by the way, before you look for a replacement, listen to a kid on your remote gang. He calls himself Barry Gray." The boss, Norman Livingston, called me within the hour and offered me the job.

I wasn't too happy about the prospect of working all night, for I'd been that route years before as a California novice. Also, I was on an ego trip. For years, in local Los Angeles radio, I'd heard smart-asses in New York sign off by saying, "This is ——— in New York. *This* is the Mutual Broadcasting System!" Now *I* was the smart-ass. Let those shit-kickers in Chillicothe and Oroville listen to a real sign-off and dream of life on the Great White Way—they'd never hear about Toffenetti's from me! But then Livingston mentioned the money the all-night chore paid. I gulped. "A hundred and seventy-five a week?" A nod from him. "Okay—but if I don't like it, can I come back to Staff?" Agreed.

I started that night.

And my "life" began.

WOR, in its "talent" change, decided to change the format of the program. There would be practically no talk, save station identification on the half hour, and this would be done musically—written, jingle-form, by a team that had enjoyed jingle success on another New York radio station. They were called Kent and Johnson, and they seemed to be the darlings of columnist Harriet Van Horne. I began my first morning of programming with a brief introduction. It was followed by a half hour of music, a jingle, then more music, then a jingle, and so on until 5:45 A.M.—and I had begun at 2 in the morning. No nights off, just music and those goddamned jingles for almost four hours. My only contact with humanity was the engineer. I would walk into the control room and we would talk about girls, his and mine. We ran out of bullshit after three days. And on the fourth I started, meagerly at first, to inject a comment on the air about a record that was about to be played. After all, I knew the bandleaders whose discs I was playing. I had announced their programs, knew them in the backstage sense. Knew their foibles, what kinds of guys they were. Had an anecdote here and there about their lives, and liked some and despised others. It was too good a forum to pass up.

My particular targets were Louis Prima, who fancied himself a stud, and Sammy Kaye, who tried. There was Vaughn Monroe, who accomplished the impossible: he sang *all* thirty-two bars of a popular song off key. Letters started to come in to the station boss. He, poor soul, lived in the suburbs and never listened to the station, and when a letter of complaint was bucked up to him, he would consult the log and reply with "You must be in error and be listening to another station. We broadcast *Moonlight Saving Time*, which is an all-music program." It was that kind of "attention" to his work which made and kept him a top executive for years.

I was not as lucky with my targets. Harriet Van Horne was furious. She loved her protégés the jingle-jokers; she hated my interruptions and so stated in her column (my boss didn't read her either—and for all I know, neither did anyone else). And Sammy Kaye and Vaughn Monroe were both in snits. Monroe threatened to punch me in the nose, but then saw the humor of the situation (or it was pointed out to him), and his record sales started to climb. He once wired me that my rapping of one particular dog he had recorded sold 45,000 copies. But Sammy Kaye, that sawdust fox, who was on the *network* air nightly immediately preceding my own program at 2, would sign off by telling people to turn their sets off, "in order to avoid hearing the insulting idiot who follows me." From coast to coast they stayed tuned, especially in the greater New York area, and enjoyed. Out of town, all they could hear was Sammy Kaye and no "idiot," so they started to complain about the program not being carried in their area. He damn near made me a star, but neither his music nor his temper got any better.

In Lindy's restaurant, then the hangout of every Broadway actor, comic, and hanger-on, the comments started about that nightly insulter on the air. Press agents told their clients what was being said. And they told columnists as well. They didn't like it. Who *was* this upstart who was taking over their racket? Giving the "inside" of the tinsel world and its people? *They* owned the turf, and they ignored me, or rapped me. I know it's difficult for a youngster to understand today the power they wielded, but they ran the town. They praised, cajoled, recommended, rapped, and criticized, and careers were made, promoted, skyrocketed, or killed overnight. Lee Mortimer, Danton Walker, Ed Sullivan, Earl Wilson, and the King, Walter Winchell, owned their beats. Lindy's, then at Broadway and 51st Street, did an enormous business during lunch and dinner, but after the theater it was *the* place to go. The famous converged on the restaurant immediately following their curtain calls, or arrived from performances at mountain resorts, or dropped in when in New York between films or out-of-town jobs. It was the late-night habitat of the celebrated, and it stayed open until 4, with certain select tables occupied by famous comics, film people, writers, columnists, and those on the fringes who gawked. A doorman kept the overflow clientele queued up outside the door awaiting admission. And at closing, many a celebrated group would stand on the corner until dawn telling stories, gossiping, and exchanging trade talk. It was the Great White Way.

And so there I sat, night after interminable night, playing the discs (or introducing them), making snide comments about the great and near-great of Broadway and Hollywood (who knew from Las Vegas then?), and working up my full quota of a dozen new enemies a night. The WOR studio I labored in, a cubicle on the twenty-fourth floor at 1440 Broadway, was almost inaccessible to the outside world. You got off an elevator, walked what seemed a full city-block corridor, then turned right, and there you were, having passed a lobby guard, elevator men, custodians, and a night manager. So I was surprised to look through the small glass window of the studio door one night to see a tiny girl, head wrapped in a bandana, peering into the studio. A record was on, so I got up and went to the door. She introduced herself, I recognized her at the same time, and I invited her to come in and join me on the air. Thus was born the guest format—ad-lib, unrehearsed, chips fall where they may. She was Carol Bruce, then a very important star on the Broadway beat, and a marvelously loquacious lady. She took off her coat and "stayed awhile"—until the program ended at 5:45, or as Damon Runyon put it "till the rosy fingers of dawn picked at the sky." After Carol's appearance and her subsequent bows in Lindy's on nights following, and her explanation that she had just "walked in," other Broadway figures began to appear, and my cubicle quickly became the new hangout for stay-up-lates.

A guest was never invited in those days. At 2 A.M. when I signed on, I had no idea whether there would be one guest, no guests, or a studioful, which would require squeezing into chairs around two microphones at a very small table. Oh, if only the acetates of those days had been made and saved of those early programs: what an anthology of postwar New York they would have made! At one sitting there would be young and vital Congressman Adam Clayton Powell, with his beautiful wife Hazel Scott. Another night, Perry Como, Jo Stafford, Frank Sinatra, George Evans (his manager), Henny Youngman, and Bernie Woods, who wrote critiques for *Variety*, the show-business bible. Joey Adams was a frequent guest, and many mornings, with the show over, we would walk home together. He lived at the Waldorf-Astoria, and I at the Belmont-Plaza across the street. We would part at the corner of 49th and Lexington. Little did I know that my $60-a-month room at the Belmont was larger than his

Waldorf digs. But then, Joey always believed in large lobbies, kings and presidents as neighbors, and a very, very small room!

About this time, when the program had been on the air but a few weeks, I had a call from Abel Green, the late editor of *Variety*. He asked if I could join him for a ride up to Harrison, New York, the following Saturday. I asked, "Why?" and he told me that Sid Silverman, the owner of *Variety*, wanted to meet me. I was impressed, and we arranged a meeting time and place, and on Saturday we went to Harrison, which to me was a world removed from Times Square (it still is).

I met Silverman in his study—a bathrobed, small, wizened man, very thin and pale, who, I later learned, was dying of tuberculosis. He was the heir to the newspaper, having inherited it from his founder father Sime Silverman, who had left a widow as well, Hattie. Sid told me that he slept little, listened to the program nightly, and had found it amusing—outrageous at times, but fresh and totally lacking in awe of the stars and sometimes stuffed shirts of the Broadway scene. He wanted to sponsor the program.

And so within a few days, *Variety* became, for the first time, the financial backer of a broadcast. And my commercials? All I did was do what I'd done for weeks before —read from *Variety* and talk about who was "wowing" them in Pittsburgh, "laying an egg" in Boston, and doing great "B.O. biz" (box-office business) in Los Angeles. Now, WOR, a 50,000-watt station, was heard throughout the Midwest and into Florida and the program was also put into the Boston area. I'll never know what effect my comments from *Variety* had on the rural population getting up early for farm chores—but it is a fact that *Variety*'s circulation climbed, and some swear the milk got richer and the eggs larger during the period of its sponsorship: about two years, if memory serves. Shortly thereafter, the paper, recognizing the growing influence of recorded music, asked me to do its first record reviews, the column to be called "Jocks and Jukes."

I wrote the column on Saturday mornings, in the record library at WOR, where I had uninterrupted access to the record players and the use of a company typewriter, and I'd drop the copy off at the Variety office on 46th Street on my way to bed. I wrote my first column and dropped it off, and was subsequently called by Abel, who invited me to the pressroom in lower Manhattan to watch it set in type, then galley-proofed and corrected, and finally put into the press run for delivery to newsstands throughout the boroughs, to trains which took it upstate, and to post offices which sent it to subscribers all over America.

It was to be a great night for me. Wow! Variety! Me —a columnist and reviewer! It was Joe Laurie, Jr., who was to be my guide and mentor in the pressroom. Laurie, a onetime headliner at the great Palace Theater, was later to become a national broadcast personality on the program Can You Top This? He took me in tow and showed me through the press plant. And finally, he picked up a galley and said, holding a lot of the set type in his hand, "Here is your column." I swelled with pride—and then Laurie lost his hold of the galley and dropped it to the floor, and type flew in every direction. I blanched, and almost cried as he said, "I don't think they can set it again in time for this edition." Then, seeing the look on my face, he laughed, as the rest of the guys in the pressroom roared, and really showed me my column. The other had been a dummy, and I had been initiated as a Variety "mugg"—a term of endearment that had been laid on by Sime and that made those who worked for the paper a very tight little commune, who wrote tough, no holds barred, about the doings on the Main Stem and were impressed only with singing elephants who sounded like Kate Smith (no analogy intended).

It was that column, which received practically no attention except from those artists reviewed, which brings to mind a couple of incidents.

As I've pointed out, the pieces were written in WOR's record library. There I could hear the program on the air, and monitor conversations of those getting ready for air as the engineers talked over the intercom with the personalities, producers, etc.

One week I couldn't write my piece on Saturday, and did it on a weekday morning. And Dorothy Kilgallen and Richard Kollmar were warming up their gargles for the most popular morning show at the time, *Breakfast with Dorothy and Dick*.

It was a religious experience, it would seem, for most of their listeners to eavesdrop on the chitchat of these noted attenders at every social event in Manhattan. She was the widely read, nationally syndicated columnist for the New York *Journal-American*, with enormous clout because of her highly touted credentials. And he was a Broadway producer, and married to Dorothy Kilgallen. They were on the air daily from their sumptuous pad on the East Side, and the engineer went to their town house every weekday morning to set up the equipment at their breakfast table so that one could hear their comments about the latest show, the newest divorce, and the expected births in the circle of the famous—this backed by the tinkle of coffee cups and comments like "Shall I pour you another cup, dear?"

New Yorkers hugged themselves with glee as they

busied themselves with oatmeal and burned toast to listen to the giddy-gadabout lives of the famous. By God, when Dorothy and Dick said it—*they were there!* But to me, their prebroadcast comments were the best part of the show—the stuff the audience never heard as the engineer fooled with his microphones and made sure all would go well. They were clearly audible to me in the record library this morning as she said to Dick, "Did you hear that son-of-a-bitch last night?"

"I did, and for my money the bastard ought be kicked off the air." The rest, for a moment or two, in the same vein, and then they were on the air. There was no doubt in my mind about their reference point—me! And that night, while I was *on the air*, I quoted the exchange. Boy! You talk about shit hitting the fan! Management had me down and banned me for life from using the speakers that would allow me to eavesdrop on the intercom, and told me in no uncertain terms that "Dorothy and Dick" were a helluva lot more important in its scheme of things than Barry Gray. I got the message. But I continued to needle them on the air gently. Just far enough, but no further—I thought.

The other experience was in finishing the column for *Variety*, and walking across Broadway and 40th Street in the early morning hours just as I heard a tremendous explosion which seemed to come from the direction of the Empire State Building on 34th Street. I hailed a cab, and was there while debris from a crashed bomber was still falling to the street. An Army plane, lost in the fog, had crashed into the Empire State Building near the top, and it was a disaster, taking its toll of life and property, which could have been much worse if the streets below had been filled with the normal quota of shoppers and 34th Street employees. Fortunately, they were nearly deserted. I rushed back to WOR and in moments had the more than 400 Mutual stations tuned in, to describe what had happened and what I'd seen. I later got a note from the boss, who wrote, "How such a schmuck could do such a good job is beyond me." Oh, he thought a lot of me! He loved me, and would continue to do so until professional death would us part—mine, not his.

The months and years passed quickly, three of them, and as I went on doing seven programs a week with guests of all shapes and sizes and opinions passing through the studio, the roster of visitors grew—and in direct proportion the number of enemies, for each guest brought his own to the microphone. One such hassle had Broadway publicist Ed Weiner making a snide comment about columnist Leonard Lyons. Lyons threatened suit, and joining him in animosity were Dorothy Kilgallen, Ed Sullivan, Danton Walker (then popular scrivener of the Daily News), and as they say, "a host of others."

WOR decided to dispense with my services. It was getting too hot in the kitchen. I must say, my support from friends was an enormous vacuum. I was fired. I was crestfallen. I was broke. I was also being given the greatest gift of my life by WOR by means of its dismissal notice, but neither of us knew it at the time. If the station's executives had known, they would have retained me, if only for making station breaks, for WOR corporate conceit is incredible, and they think no one recovers from their dismissal!

With about a week to go before I ended my tenure at the station, my phone rang in the apartment. It was John Pransky calling. Pransky was a booker of Borsht Belt acts and with his partner, Al Beckman, had cornered the market in that field. They booked talent into dozens of hotels throughout the Catskills, and they were calling to find if I knew where a certain actor was, for they wanted to reach him. I didn't know, and Pransky casually inquired, "What're you up to?" I said, "Nothing, Johnny—you know that WOR fired me?" There was a brief silence at the other end, and then he said, "Hold the phone a minute." I could tell he'd muffled the phone with his hand and was speaking rapidly to someone in the room with him. He came back to the phone and asked, "Where are ya now?" I said, "Home—the Ruxton, at 72nd and Columbus." He said, "We'll be right over!" And hung up. "We'll be right over"? Who was "we"?

In about ten minutes there was a knock at the door, and Pransky stood there with the "we"—another man. He introduced him quickly as "Murray Weinger, the owner of the Copacabana in Miami Beach." Weinger asked if I would like to come to Miami Beach and do a broadcast from the lounge. His was the best club in the Dade County area. In the big room they booked Hildegarde, Berle, Chevalier, and a great roster of stars. Adjoining that room was a lounge. It seated about 200, and currently was just a quiet bar. Weinger wanted to put it to use. For transportation plus $200 per week on a firm four-week contract. I agreed and immediately got $500 "railroad money." I was to open on September 30, 1947. In the main room would be Hildegarde. I would be in the lounge. My wife, Beth, and I arrived with paper suitcases a couple of days before the opening and checked into the Hotel Atlantis pending finding permanent quarters, and that would happen only if at the end of four weeks I was retained.

Two and a half years later, I had all my worldly possessions packed to be shipped back to New York, and I was being moved from fashionable Pinetree Drive to the Hampshire House in Manhattan—a long way from the Atlantis Hotel on the Beach.

In the intervening three seasons the program had not only become a long-running hit on the Beach, but had been turning away crowds nightly. It had also taken on a political aura, for those were the days of the Senator Claude Pepper–Congressman George Smathers fight for Pepper's Senate seat. Pepper lost. They were both on my program, which was conducted originally from a slightly raised dais in the lounge.

One night after the place had closed (my broadcast was from midnight until 3 on WKAT Miami Beach, then a Mutual affiliate), I was sitting in the Mammy's Hangout restaurant for stay-up-lates on the Beach when a guy ran in and yelled, "The Copa's on fire!" I rushed to the club, and sure enough, the fire was raging out of control as a wind whipped the blaze, and firemen rushed into and out of the liquor supply room with bulges under their coats. The few who had hoses on the flame (I surmised they would divvy the liquor take later) were "fighting" the blaze in a most unorthodox manner. They were playing water on the fire, it seemed to me, to enlarge it, rather than contain it. And why not?—I had become the "nigger lover" of the Southern broadcast bands. I had clamored for civil rights in a town that made its blacks carry identification cards. They had been allowed on the Beach, if they worked there, only after dark. They traveled to work in jitneys for blacks only. And they did not live there. Entertainers who were black, no matter how great their success up North, could not work on the Beach, but were restricted to a black club on the Miami side, called the Harlem Square Club. And some of America's most noted black talents appeared there, but had not been able to cross Biscayne Bay and buy a drink, or see a friend on the "white side" of the causeway linking the Beach with the mainland. Even my boss, paying deferential attention to New York broadcast opinions on the state of the State, referred to them as "Nigras."

Over in Miami, Bill "Bojangles" Robinson was appearing. It was his birthday. I had invited every white star on the Beach to join me in a pilgrimage to Robinson's club to pay him honor. I had gathered up Sophie Tucker, Harry Richman, Jackie Miles, Joe E. Lewis, Maurice Chevalier, Milton Berle, and every other star I could find; walked into a club wall-to-wall with black patrons; and tendered Robinson the tribute of his life. Tears had run freely. I had had the privilege of emceeing the event, and I had asked Bill publicly to come to broadcast with me the following week. The next day, the show the night before, and my invitation, had been the talk of the beach. The night he appeared, every police officer and deputy sheriff in the area had surrounded the Copa. It had been an armed camp, for threats of violence had been received in every mail and via the telephone. But when Robinson had walked into the club through a cordon of cops, hundreds of Copa patrons had given him a standing ovation. Weinger, the Copa owner, had seen this, and Miami Beach Jim Crow had started dying that night.

Within a short space of time, the Step Brothers, a team of four incredibly gifted dancers, had appeared as the stars of the Copa show, and *lived* on the Beach. The threats had continued, as antiblack policies rocketed to the left and right. And then the fire. It had been expected. By now I had begun to carry a gun just to go home at night. I cased the block via car before I parked to get out, and then, gun drawn, would walk quickly into my apartment. It sounds melodramatic, but it was a time of violence. Of course, a quarter of a century after the fact, the gun seems useless: if you're marked for a "hit," relax and "enjoy it," for professionals need only a moment to wreak grievous harm or death on their victim— but that's another chapter.

And so the Copa burned, and the next night, in lieu of the regular broadcast from inside the poshest club in the South, I did my program from the sidewalk alongside the charred ruins on WKAT, and simultaneously, through a public-address system, it was carried for half a mile in every direction as thousands of the curious, the fans and foes, turned out to see what we would do without stage, napery, obsequious waiters, and name entertainment. Weinger immediately set to work to build a new and finer club. He retained the famous architect Norman Bel Geddes to draw the plans, and put me into the Lord Tarleton Hotel on a lend-lease basis until the new club was ready. I passed the spring, summer and most of the fall of that year in the Tarleton. By now my income had grown to ten times the original figure. But it made little difference. My life-style accepted every advance with aplomb. If I made $2,000 per week, I needed $2,500. It was so easy to buy things.

Then the new Copacabana was ready. It was like an enormous gorgeous girl. It was big—tremendous; flossy, comfortable, dimly lit; a main room that seated over 1,000, a lounge that held 400, a snakelike bar which took up one end of the lounge and where a couple of hundred more could nurse a drink and watch the goings-on. Broadcast time was extended an hour—now four hours, from midnight until 4 A.M., and never a dull moment. At a given hour you might find Danny Kaye, Martin and Lewis, and Carmen Miranda all on the air together. Or the Ritz Brothers, Joe E. Lewis, Jackie Miles, "Fat Jack" Leonard, and Danny Thomas all trading jokes and insults over the air, which were heard and seen by those in attendance at the Copa.

It was a wonderful season. A great year for the grape, 1949, and a wonderful, recallable year for me. God grant it would never end—but of course, it did, and 1950 rolled in. Weinger started to draw the interest of the Internal Revenue Service—something about undeclared profits. Coincidentally, I received an inquiry from a Lou Rubin about coming back to New York, to his place called Chandler's, on East 46th Street, just off Lexington. The Copa, almost overnight, was shuttered by the IRS, and I left Miami Beach in April 1950 to drive to California to visit my parents, brother, and sisters, and planned to arrive in New York for an opening at Chandler's on May 15, 1950. I had gone to the Beach in '47 with a fairly new wife, a brand-new daughter, borrowed money, suitcases tied with rope, and two suits. I was leaving in 1950 in a brand-new Cadillac and with a helluva wardrobe; my wife was dripping in furs (it's cool at night) and good jewelry; and our bags were matching leather. Christ! What a land of opportunity this is!

I arrived in New York about four days in advance of my "debut" at Chandler's and met almost at once with Lou Rubin, who told me that every radio station in town had turned down the proposal to broadcast from his restaurant nightly from midnight until 3. They were evasive; they didn't want to "run all night," and in one case, "Barry Gray is too controversial." That last came from Norman Boggs, then the general manager of WMCA. It angered me, for Boggs was listening to gossip rather than ascertaining fact, and I called him and asked for a meeting. He agreed. And with Rubin we met on Friday afternoon, before the advertised opening on the Monday night following. The ads had been placed in the papers, the columns (those that would print it—Earl Wilson and some Long Island scribes) had noted my return, and we had no radio station to carry the show. Rubin said, "I don't care if we can't get a station; you'll sit on the dais and talk to the customers!"

The Boggs meeting started off with his lengthy speech about station policy, the fact that WMCA had been going off the air at midnight, and what amounted to a crock of evasive *merde*. When he paused for breath, I asked what he had been getting for commercials on the late-night air, prior to closing. He said, "Five dollars, when we can." I pointed out that in Miami Beach, where one-minute commercial announcements sold for a dollar a night, our rates for the Copa's shows were $20 a spot, and we were carrying 32 commercials in a four-hour stint, seven nights a week. Boggs got a gleam in his eye—one signifying pure hunger. He asked, "What do ya think a spot would go for here?" I said, "Forty dollars." He said, "Well, we'll have to keep three engineers on duty [one with me, one at the studio, and one at the transmitter], and there will be other incidental expenses. What kind of a guarantee can we have to cover those costs for thirteen weeks—your first cycle?"

Rubin and I looked at each other. He had agreed to pay me $1,000 per week, and I was to divide any commercial money with him. If the show was a hit he figured to have the program for nothing, and all the food and beverages he sold during the show would be pure gravy. I asked Boggs, "What kind of guarantee do you want?" He said, "How about eight hundred fifty a week?"—for he never believed, as he said later, that there would be a quarter coming in from commercials. I agreed, and in so doing, I was immediately working for $150 a week ($850 from $1,000) and half of any commercial money that came in, which I was to split with Rubin.

I opened on Monday. Over the weekend, merchants who had heard the show in Miami Beach and visited the Copa climbed on board, and on opening night there were 16 commercial sponsors on the show at $40 per night, seven nights a week, and the guarantee, from that day until this, was never paid. Within two weeks, with me playing to a packed saloon nightly, Rubin tore up my old contract and upped the ante to $1,250 and a 26-week deal. Two weeks later, he went to $1,500 and a 39-week deal. And two weeks later he made it an even $2,000 per week and signed me for a firm year. That was 1950, and those were pretty impressive figures in that period—not to be sneezed at even today. Within the year I was also doing a nightly 11 P.M. news-and-comment quarter hour on Channel 5 television, sponsored by Sealy Mattress; appearing every Saturday night with Steve Allen on the CBS network *Songs for Sale* (the panel changed weekly, but I remained), and emceeing an afternoon quiz show for Goodson-Todman called *Winner Take All*. In my "spare time" I lectured on everything from V.D. among the natives of the Upper Volta to "the vagaries of a checkered existence as propounded by B. S. Pully."

But about my opening night at Chandler's, May 15, 1950. Every comic I had known and loved in Miami Beach was there, and in the front row of a restaurant that seated just under 300 patrons were Milton Berle, Danny Thomas, Jan Murray, Phil Foster, and Jackie Miles, to name just a few. Phil Foster asked to be on first. I agreed, for I loved his salty, sawtoothed humor. After my opening comments—"It's good to be back in New York, happy to see the large turnout," etcetera—I introduced Foster, who came to the tiny dais and promptly attacked every comic in the room for stealing his material. The comics were livid, they fought for a place at the microphones (there were three), and their screaming insults to Foster continued until the show went off the air. That night in Lindy's the program was subject matter at every table, and the discussions continued into the next day, and the day after that, and the day after that—in short, the program was controversially off, running, and a solid hit!

In the months that followed, every name of Broadway, Hollywood, and Washington appeared. Irving Berlin came to sing his songs, accompanied by the Three Suns. They ran to their apartment to grab their instruments when Berlin was cajoled into song. Danny Thomas pontificated almost nightly; Berle brought his mother, Sandra, to tell of her life bringing "Uncle Miltie" along from childhood to international stardom. The room was narrow and long, and there was a room-wide bar in the back. At every table there were cards that prompted the patrons to send a note up to a guest on the air, or me. It was the midnight *Town Hall of the Air*. We had discussions of the German war trials, with former Army prosecutor Moses Kove (now New York's taxi commissioner) telling us in detail of the life and deaths of the Nazi scum. Kay Armen would sing a *cappella* to a standing ovation. There were movie producers, movie stars (Grace Kelly one of them—plugging her appearance in *High Noon*), mayors (Vincent Impellitteri) from every town within earshot of WMCA, Senators, sinners, and sycophants.

It was a ball! The show was in its third year—and had reached the point where the doorman would open the door of a cab or limousine when it pulled up under the Chandler's awning to ask its occupants, "Do you have a reservation?" If the answer was no, they were told it was too bad, but seats were not available. A velvet rope kept the crowd back as we neared air time, and no guest was ever invited. The celebrities just dropped in, and were spotted by my assistant, Herb Lanzet, who would scribble a note to tell me who had entered the room, for the dais was brightly lit and I could see only two or three rows back. Some nights I would apologize to eight or ten prominent guests for not having any more air time and therefore being not able to have them on. It looked as though we were having the longest-running hit on Broadway.

And then, on a night in 1952, Josephine Baker walked into the room. She had been the internationally acclaimed star of Paris' *Folies Bergère*. She was in New York briefly, and that night she came into Chandler's about five minutes before we were to go off the air. I recognized her at once, but gestured at my watch to let her know that time was practically gone, and I could not have her on the air. She nodded, smiled, and made a sign to have me join her table when I finished.

I did.

And she told me that she had just come from the Stork Club minutes before. She had gone there in the company of an actor who was Ezio Pinza's standby in *South Pacific*. That show was then the outstanding hit on Broadway. At the Stork Club, they had been made to wait for a table before they were finally seated. They had sat, she said, at a table adjoining Walter Winchell's. They had waited for service for more than half an hour. She had realized that she was being avoided by waiters, captains, and management. She was furious. And her anger was aimed at Winchell, for he, she said, was "the great liberal—and did nothing to have his friend Sherman Billingsley intervene and see that I was accorded proper treatment." She had left the club in a fury and had come to Chandler's to tell her story and attack Winchell.

I didn't know what to do. Winchell had befriended me in my initial job at WOR. He would stop by when I got off the air, and in the company of Damon Runyon we would cruise the city's streets, chasing police calls and watching the city awaken for the day, and then adjourn to Reuben's, then *the* all-night restaurant of Manhattan, and Winchell would talk, and I would listen, hanging on every word.

I couldn't believe that *the* Walter Winchell, he who traveled with kings and presidents, and addressed millions of Americans every Sunday night on his *Jergens Journal* (the hand lotion) would seek me out, and talk, and talk, and talk. That was one thing you had to be in his company—a listener. For Winchell had a lot to say, and he said it—by the hour. Runyon would scribble notes, most of them put-downs of Winchell—for Runyon by then had lost his voice as a result of an operation for throat cancer. His days were numbered.

Winchell had not offered advice or solace when I got fired at WOR, and his column had often mentioned me as the all-night smart-ass. But he had helped me along, and he did surface again in Florida, where he wintered at the Roney Plaza, and would drop into the Copa often to listen, scribble me notes while I was on the air, and in general let management know that I was very much in his favor. It hadn't hurt.

It is impossible to re-create for America's young the

power of the Winchell press in those years, the late forties and early fifties, but if he mentioned an act, it immediately got star billing and more work than it could handle. A girl in a chorus line would be singled out for mention, and she would be feted and screen-tested. The reverse was also true. If Winchell disliked you and wrote about it, the best thing you could do would be find a high window, or a handful of sleeping pills. Don't put it down—many a career ended, and a life, because of Winchell.

His was the power and the glory. He wrote for hundreds of newspapers a week; he broadcast to millions every Sunday night. He was a product of that America. He rubbed elbows with mob guys and J. Edgar Hoover (whom he idolized); he was the go-between of the underworld and law enforcement. Originally a small-time hoofer in vaudeville, he had climbed to the top of the heap with a column that could send stocks up, careers down, and influence every level of our thinking during his reign. One item he carried about a New York beauty which stated she was "infanticipating" (Winchellese for expecting a baby) gave the date of the baby's arrival nine months thereafter. One Broadwayite said (quietly), "She must've called Walter as soon as she got out of bed!"

To put Josephine Baker on the air would surely incur his wrath—unless I called him and asked him to come on to refute the charges. I called; he had left for Florida, I was told, and was unreachable. I sent him a telegram. I then asked Josephine Baker to return the following night with her attorney, who was Arthur Garfield Hays, a noted, respected civil libertarian, and with Hays at her side, Josephine Baker could tell her story. I wanted to make sure that her comments would not constitute the basis of a lawsuit, in which, by law, I would be joined—for they were WMCA microphones, and I was the station's "keeper of the keys" after midnight.

Miss Baker appeared the following night as scheduled. The Broadway day was buzzing with news of her expected appearance and what had happened at the Stork Club. Reporters had already picked it up, and it was front page, and highlighted Earl Wilson's column. The city was primed and waiting for the Baker comments on l'affaire Stork. That night I introduced her and her attorney. She told in a straightforward manner the story of her brush-off at the Stork. And she then lashed into Winchell for his seeming indifference to her presence and problem. Her portion of the program ended, and I went on with business as usual—comics, politicians, and a lady who danced with birds.

The next day I attempted again to get Winchell or his spokesman to come on the air. I was successful in getting boxing champion "Sugar Ray" Robinson and publicist Ed Weiner (a Winchell aide) to appear. They offered a rather pallid defense of their chief. They didn't refute any of the Baker charges, but rather talked of Walter's great attacks in the cause of civil rights.

When the program was over, I was handed a copy of the *Daily Mirror* (Winchell's flagship newspaper). The attacks on Baker had begun. She was accused of selling out to the Nazis when France was occupied by the Wehrmacht. She was a "traitor to America" because she lived abroad. And, as I recall, he said her act wasn't too good in the first place.

Josephine Baker requested another appearance at the mikes. She came on, and quietly put to rest (I thought) the Winchell charges. She showed the audience a medal given to her by the De Gaulle Free French Forces for efforts in their behalf. She told of her love for America, but said that her work had received great acclaim in Paris, and like most performers, she went where the work was—and in short, she acquitted herself admirably. She left the dais to the cheers of the audience.

Immediately after her appearance, I was called to the phone. It was Ed Sullivan, the New York *Daily News* columnist. He asked to come on the air "to defend Josephine Baker." I agreed, and told him that Winchell had been invited, and would be invited again. He said, "It makes no difference—I want to talk about that lady, and tomorrow night, if possible!" I went back to the microphones (taken over for a few minutes by a celebrity guest in the restaurant) and recounted my conversation with Sullivan. The people in the audience gasped, for they had heard the stories of the Winchell–Sullivan feud over the years. Of Sullivan grabbing Winchell's tie one night in a popular restaurant after Winchell had greeted him and telling him, in a fury, "If you ever talk to me again, you son-of-a-bitch, I'll beat you to a pulp."

I wired Winchell at the Roney Plaza in Florida. Either him, or a spokesman. The fires were growing hotter. No response.

The night Sullivan appeared, Chandler's walls seemed bent from the crowd within. There wasn't an inch of space as he walked to the dais. His comments were recorded on acetate. I've always found them so fascinating, particularly in view of what took place later, that I intended to reprint the entire transcript of what was said right here, at this point in the book. My editor thought that would be a mistake, arguing that it would interrupt the flow of my own story for much too long, and particularly when the reader, hopefully, was just getting interested in Barry Gray. His advice was to capsule Sullivan's remarks briefly here, so that the reader would understand what the entire episode was all about, and shift the full 16 pages required to print the complete transcript of the acetate recording to the end of my book, as a sort of appendix. That way the reader could choose whether to look at it later or turn to it now. (For those in the latter category, it starts on page 176.)

I still don't know if my editor was right or not. But how often does an author win an argument with an editor? So (for those in the first category), here's the gist of Sullivan's remarks.

After complimenting me for conducting a completely open forum on controversial topics, he told of his liberal record dating back years before this date, when he had agreed to be drawn into the Winchell–Josephine Baker case. As a young sportswriter 24 years earlier, he had written about the villainy of humiliating a Negro football player when his team was scheduled to face a Southern university's team. He called Walter Winchell evil and treacherous, and said he despised him, but added that he was appreciative of being on a stand where Winchell could, if he desired, retort and answer him. Sullivan talked of his contributions and fights over two decades for the underprivileged or despised minorities: Negroes, Jews, Italians, Irish Catholics, the Nisei, whoever. Then he went into the Josephine Baker matter specifically, denouncing Winchell again and again with passion, and saying how gratified he was to be able to stand up with me to help take up the fight. I responded in kind, and that's the capsule version.

Within a day or two after Sullivan's comments, Beth and I went to Europe on vacation. For a period of three weeks. A visit to Paris; the train to Vienna, then under the four-power trust agreement (when we arrived, the

Russians were in power); and then back to Paris to meet with Broadway producer Leland Hayward, his wife Slim, Louis Jourdan, Billy Wilder, and some other very notable people at a lunch at Maxim's.

The great old ship the *Queen Elizabeth* brought us back to New York. Shipboard companions made it a memorable crossing: Moss Hart and Kitty Carlisle, Bernard Baruch, Edna Ferber, Aly Khan, shoe designer David Evins, Gertrude Berg ("Molly Goldberg"), and Tex Ritter, the cowboy star. The ship docked in New York in the early morning hours of an August day. Comic Jack Carter and his wife, Joan, brought us the current issue of the *Daily Mirror*. The Winchell attacks on me had started.

They continued for three years. I was (and sometimes in the same column) a Fascist, a Communist, a heterosexual, a homosexual, a marital cheater, a deadbeat, a lousy broadcaster, and un-American. With a play on my name (legally changed when I was in my late teens) I was "Borey Pink," "Borey Yellow," "Borey Red," etc. It was total war, and Winchell was doing a first-rate job on all fronts. He had an ally—Senator Joseph McCarthy, who had heard the sounds of my wrath nightly on Channel 5, during the commentary period of the program, and again on WMCA. McCarthy called for, and got, my income-tax returns. He could do nothing with them, for I'd paid all my taxes, but by God, he tried (I've been audited every year by the IRS since McCarthy started his illegal search and seizure).

The first result of the Winchell attack (helped by McCarthy) was the cancellation of my 11 P.M. news program. It was sponsored by Sealy Mattress—whose executives turned to pure Jell-O during the period. WABD Channel 5, during the Army–McCarthy hearings, insisted on script approval before I could do my narrative of the day's events. Because the hearings ended very late in the day, it would have been impossible to have a script written and polished in time for airing. What I did, in fact, was give the hard news, reading off a TelePrompTer, and then, without notes, do a roundup of what I'd seen and heard during the McCarthy–Welch exchanges. I was an angry but slanderproof man, for I was on solid ground, using truth as my defense.

The general manager of Channel 5 was a McCarthy admirer (he's long gone), and it was he who writhed at my nightly dissertations on, and dissections of, the see-through Senator from Wisconsin. The station canceled my contract, which had some six months to run. Sealy Mattress said, "Even though you *have* grounds for a lawsuit, don't do it—why be a troublemaker?" I allowed myself to be persuaded. After the fact, I realized I had been a fool. The whole sorry mess would have embarrassed Sealy and put Channel 5's license in jeopardy, but the attendant publicity would have smoked out some conspiratorial rats.

Winchell gloated—and had more fun with my name. He seemed maniacal on the subject. Through press agents, he pressured guests against coming on my program. One agent, Jack Beekman, told me straight, "I won't allow my people to go on with you; you're too hot —and I need Winchell." One of his people, singer Kay Armen, a lady with a glorious voice, had not only been a guest of mine often, but sat in for me on numerous occasions—during a period of illness, vacation, etc. Another, Fred Robbins, who had attained some fame as the pivotal figure of his program *Robbins' Nest*, had been my friend for years. We had dinner together with our wives one Sunday night, and on Monday I talked about the great suburban restaurant where we had dined on the air. Freddie called to thank me for not mentioning his name, because of Winchell. I listened, aghast at his comment, and replied, "You cowardly son-of-a-bitch!" We didn't speak for almost a decade.

Sponsors started to disappear one by one as Winchell's legion of pimps got the word around that their support of me made him "very unhappy." Who knew what Government inspection they might incur through his wrath? Yes, he *had* that kind of power. But the one power he didn't have was to oust me from WMCA. He made a fatal error—the mistake of overkill. He dubbed the station's call letters as meaning "We Make Communists Adorable." The late Nathan Straus, who owned the shop, decreed, in livid anger, that "if Barry has *no* sponsors he stays on the air!"

It never got quite that bad, but the nature of the show did change. Where the great and near-great had rushed down to Chandler's nightly to be seen or heard, their names were now suddenly unspoken on the air, for they weren't there. No more Danny Thomas with his nightly homilies. Danny, who drove to my home one rainy day to look down at the floor and tell me his agency had advised him not to go on the air with me—I was too hot! Danny said, "What am I supposed to do—do my act and then pause and say I'd like to say a few words about my friend Barry Gray? Winchell would murder me!" I didn't reply, but merely walked him to my door. It was more than a decade before we spoke on the air again—and it was never the same. He had turned yellow—and we both knew it. But so did so many others—Jan Murray, Phil Foster, Jack E. Leonard, Sophie Tucker, and in fact, anyone who was on top—for they all feared Winchell. He literally carried a gun in his pocket, and figuratively one in his typewriter.

Where earlier I had walked into Lindy's and greeted friends left and right, now a visit to Lindy's became *High Noon*: conversation would cease as all eyes watched to see who would say hello. Only one person did. He got up from his table on the far wall, walked the full, horizontal length of the restaurant, and welcomed me warmly —and loudly. Danny Kaye was a real Gary Cooper!

I started to get an unusual amount of crank mail. And one night a man who frequented Chandler's and who I suspected had mob connections told me a "small contract" had been put out on me. I couldn't believe it. This was America! What had I done but put Josephine Baker and Ed Sullivan on the air?

A few nights later, in the company of a writer pal, "Snag" Werris, I stopped at Longchamps, then at 58th Street and Madison Avenue, where the General Motors Building is today. I repaired to the washroom, and as I stood at the urinal, a greasy-looking guy came in, saw me, quickly rinsed his hands, and left the room. After I'd washed mine, I walked out, and he was sitting in a phone booth furtively talking with someone at the other end. I went upstairs, we ate, and then we walked to Snag's car on the opposite curb. My hands were filled with books, magazines, and mail—my homework for the night.

As Snag entered the car on the driver's side, I walked around to the other door of the car and waited for him to lean across and open the lock for me. I heard a quick scuff of a shoe behind me. As I turned to see what it was, I caught a haymaker in the eye, and went down for the count. Snag, now turning to open the door for me, didn't see me—but did see three men kicking something out of his line of sight, below the level of the car door. I was being worked over—in the ribs, groin, head, face— but fortunately didn't feel it, for I was unconscious. He yelled, "What're you doing?" and leaped out of the car to run around to the sidewalk. One man pulled a gun and said, "Stay out of this, you bastard." They jumped into a car and took off. Snag brought me to, and we went to the police station to make a report.

The next day the *New York Post* carried a full-front-page picture of me with bruises, cuts, and a gorgeous black eye. Winchell had that picture framed, and put the blowup over his bed at the St. Moritz Hotel. The cops put two bodyguards on me and started their investigation. But they seemed to know where it would lead them, and dragged their feet. It seemed to me they were much more interested in preventing another attack than in tracing the perpetrators of the past one.

It was during the day following the working-over that the doorbell rang at my apartment. I was lying down, nursing the badly blackened eye and my bone injuries with compresses. My daughter, then about 5, answered the bell and, on opening the door, saw a tall, slim stranger wearing a well-tailored gray suit, very natty in appearance. He looked down and said, "Miss, is your daddy at home?" With that, Melodie turned and yelled, "Daddy, a cop is here to see you!" The stranger started to laugh, and as I came to the door to invite him in, he said, "I've been a cop for twenty-five years, and never got 'made' so fast."

He was Lieutenant Frank Robb of the New York Police Department. We became good friends. But we both knew the job had been pulled by professionals, and it would be a fruitless hunt—in fact, the hoodlums were by now probably far out of town. What we would concern ourselves with would be avoiding a repetition of the attack. He wanted to know if I knew of anyone who might want me worked over. My reply gave rise to Earl Wilson's comment that "the suspect list has narrowed to 1,000."

Although having a two-man police bodyguard team sounds wonderful, in practice it is horrendous! They ate with me, went to work with me, picked me up whenever I left the apartment, put me back into the apartment at day's end; in short, I was blanketed—no, suffocated—by their presence, although they were good guys just doing their job. And could they eat! At the end of about three months, I had had it. It was too much. And besides, we had decided to move to Westchester, so the bodyguard was withdrawn. The police also insisted I carry a gun. A .38-caliber Colt. I became proficient with it and prayed I'd never have to use it.

By now the fall season had come, and one night I was on my way to DuMont Television down at the old John Wanamaker building. It was 10 o'clock. And as I walked across the street to enter the studios, three guys came flying around the corner. I barely noticed them, for there was a bus stop on the next corner, and many times people ran for the bus. As they came opposite me, my back was to them. Suddenly, I was belted across the back of the head with some hard, metallic object; knocked down; again kicked repeatedly; and then left in a semihaze as they took off as swiftly as they'd come. The police came ultimately with the same questions, the same routine. And the same feeling of helplessness about finding the culprits. A metal bar was found in a gutter nearby; no other clues.

We moved to Westchester. The New York Police Department reassigned me a bodyguard, only now the officers accompanied me to my car and tailed me to the first tollbooth near the George Washington Bridge; at that point the Westchester Highway Police took over, and tailed me to the Weaver Street exit of the Hutchinson River Parkway; and there the New Rochelle Police picked up the trail, put me into my driveway, and waited until I entered the house and they saw, through a series of preplanned light patterns, that all was well. Then they took off, but many times during the night I would hear their car quietly cruising the street. That too began to be oppressive after a while. I felt more caged than protected, so I asked them to call it off. After all, I did live in a rather isolated area, and it would be nearly impossible for anyone to "sneak up on me." And I had a gun.

I carried it (it was now winter) unholstered and loose in my right overcoat pocket. I arrived in my driveway about 4 one morning. It was quite dark, and with a load of books and papers under my left arm, I got out of the car and put my right hand into my coat pocket to grip the gun until I reached my front door. Midway up the walk across the lawn, I heard a man ask, out of the darkness, "Barry Gray?" With that, I pulled the gun from my pocket, and holding it behind my left arm and its load of books, I said, "Yes." He quickly said, "I'm sorry to disturb you, but I'm one of your neighbors, and I wanted to tell you how much I enjoyed your programs!" I thanked him and went into the house and started to shake. He had been an instant away from being shot, and I would have been guilty of shooting an innocent man. Nothing would have been worth it. The next day, I walked into the West 54th Street precinct and turned in my gun and permit. Let them slug away. I would never carry a gun again!

Meanwhile, *Winchell* was slugging away. Daily in his

column, a diatribe. He gave my home address in West-chester, so that the mailed filth of diseased minds might be sent to me directly—like *used* toilet tissue. There were threats by mail, strangers slowly driving past the house. In short, a period of harassment that one who has not been through it can hardly imagine! My income dropped precipitously, the phone stopped ringing, the invitations for cocktails ceased, and the doorbell never was pressed by a guest. It was the war of nerves I'd been told to expect but could not have imagined. What gave me the longest pause for thought, however, was the total silence from Ed Sullivan's quarter, and from Josephine Baker.

Following Sullivan's brave proclamation on the air, and during his attack on Winchell in which he said he had told me "that if he [I] ever wanted me to fill in any spot on his program, if ever there was an occasion when he didn't have enough guests—he always has them—but if ever the occasion arose that he didn't have 'em, to please call me up. That as an American, I would be very proud to come here and help him out for a magnificent American job that he has done here at this microphone," I was told by one of the *Daily News* Annenbergs that Sullivan would not write a line about the Winchell–Baker fracas in his column, and if I was expecting help from his quarter to forget it. I asked why. And was told, " 'Cause we [the *Daily News*] won't let him!"

I couldn't believe that, but when the heat was on I telephoned Sullivan at his Hotel Delmonico suite and asked his man Carmen to have Sullivan give me a call. I wanted to update Ed on the pressures against guests, sponsors, and station by Winchell and his mercenaries. No call from Sullivan came. I did this for some weeks, and then one night I bumped into Benny Gaines, a well-to-do realtor from Miami Beach, who was very close to Sullivan. I told Benny of my repeated unsuccessful attempts to reach the columnist. His advice to me was simply—"Keep your chin up." The rest, to quote an earlier chronicler, was silence. I did not see or hear from Sullivan for about six or seven years.

By then Chandler's had been hit with an OPA edict, which among other things threatened and later did impose an entertainment tax because of my broadcast. I voluntarily moved from there, over Rubin's protestations (we are still friends), and took the microphone to the Shelton Hotel—it had a lounge that seemed perfect for the program. It wasn't. Then it was off to the Delmonico Hotel (with Sullivan living upstairs, although I never saw him, nor did he call), and it too was a quick charade, and a mockery of what the exciting Chandler's shows had been. And we were now *inviting* guests, and getting more turndowns than acceptances. Suddenly, an epidemic of colds, prior engagements, "just leaving town," and "he's out of town" broke out in answer to our invitations. And I found myself, more and more, talking with political guests, who couldn't have cared less about Winchell— all they wanted was to be elected—and guests with a human-interest story. Good radio fare, but hardly entertainment for a lounge, where people wanted to see celebrities. I was "playing" to empty tables.

I put the program into the WMCA studios, then just three floors over Lindy's at 51st and Broadway. We had a studio audience. And I must add, on a first-come, first-served basis (no tickets), people were turned away nightly. It did provide problems, for we didn't have proper studio personnel to police the area. I worked in a large studio, with an audience of perhaps 100. Sometimes a malcontent would be among them (why not?), and once one of them became so disenchanted with the program that he defecated in a quiet hallway near the studio. I must say his was forceful criticism.

The months went by and a restaurant named Hutton's called me. It had tried the radio talk/celebrity format with Henry Morgan, Eva Gabor, Laraine Day, and others, and struck out each time. Hutton's was just up the block from Chandler's, and I decided to go in there on a percentage basis: a cut of the gross between 11 at night and the closing for the night. It was one of many foolish business decisions I've made. Week after week the place was filled, with perhaps an empty table or two on a Monday night. And the patrons ate and drank, I thought, in a festive mood. Each Saturday my check for the preceding week was minute in comparison with what I thought it should be, and I was told, "Big crowd, but they didn't drink"—or "Didn't have too many customers this week." I was too stupid to call in my own auditor, and anyway, we were coming up to New Year's Eve. With a fixed-price policy. Fifteen dollars per person pre-inflation, with hats, horns, food, and a bottle of champagne on the table, all other beverages extra. The place was packed from bar to dais. Not an inch of room. And when payday came, the check was lower than ever. I had been taken—royally. And I quit, and went back into the studio. And there I remained for some time, sans an audience, glad, in many ways, not to be diverted by outside influences. From time to time I would try other saloons, but within days I was bored with the atmosphere and the pressure of coming up with "celebrity names"—or being in the middle of a particularly informative interview only to see a party of eight getting up to leave. It was disconcerting.

For brief periods I broadcast from Bob Olin's (he was

once a leading boxer) on Central Park West, in the place now called Stampler's. I worked at Ben Maksik's Town and Country Club in Brooklyn. That required me to drive over an hour to get there, and we arranged a limousine service to pick up the guests and "shlep" them to the program. And for a period of six weeks, in the height of the winter season, I originated from the Seville Hotel in Miami Beach, feeding the program to WMCA in New York and thence to the entire Mutual network. It was a fluke, that network, for I borrowed Gabriel Heatter's long line. He lived in Miami Beach, delivered his "good news" each night from there, and paid for the telephone line that carried his program to Master Control in New York (WOR), which sent it out to the nation. He was an old, good friend. Briefly I had been his announcer when I came out of the Army, and he lent me his long line, and Mutual figured, What the hell: "we have nothing else to put on at this hour; may as well let Gray have his sandpile."

When that period in Miami Beach concluded, I returned to the Town and Country Club, and little realized that I was about to terminate my saloon broadcast career abruptly. Although I worked with great stars visiting from the main room, and the guest problem was beginning to ease, I didn't care for the Town and Country's carnival atmosphere, despite its being a beautiful club. By now, incidentally, Winchell was on television a half hour a week, and the show was terrible. The King's crown was slipping. He would do his familiar "Good evening, Mr. and Mrs. North America and all the ships at sea" opening, then introduce his guests who would perform, while a jury box filled with well-known personalities would be introduced to watch and comment. It was terrible.

One incident comes to mind. Henny Youngman was the star of the show at Ben Maksik's in Brooklyn, and I was in the lounge. All the others stars who appeared in that main room had come on to me almost nightly—Tony Bennett, the Ritz Brothers, Tony Martin, Jackie Cannon. But Youngman told me he couldn't do it, for he was up for a booking on the Winchell show and didn't want to "blow it." He was on the Winchell show, and you can see how far he's progressed since. But one night I was talking with a national political figure, and I had just asked him how he felt about recognition of Red China (this was the late fifties)—and in the split second of silence before he replied, a male voice was heard to say, "Shall we go to my place or yours?" It was a three-minute laugh, and I knew then that saloons would never again be for me.

Meanwhile, in the deepest crevices of Yellow Journalism, plans were being hatched for a new monthly called *Confidential*. Rumor had it that its publisher, who shall remain nameless, for he has sunk into personal oblivion, was being financed by Winchell. It would certainly seem so, for each day, in the weeks preceding the issuance of the first edition, Winchell plugged its arrival daily and saturated his column with innuendos about the great "inside" story it would print on "Borey Pink, Yellow, and Lavender."

When the issue arrived, it was snapped off the newsstands as a collector's item. The great story? First, a cover picture, the same one that had appeared on the *New York Post*, showing me with a shiner, and inside, the "big" story that I had a "large" collection of cuff links (I own about eight pairs). It was as fraudulent as all else he said, but his henchmen worked ceaselessly on every outlet they could find. And again, if it had not been for Nathan Straus, I'm sure my broadcast career would have ended.

The pride that came out of the period was that I never asked for quarter, and after getting the "message" from Ed Sullivan, I ceased wondering where everyone had gone. The trick was simply to stay alive. I received opportunities during that time to work in Rome, London, and California, and often wanted to go, for a variety of reasons. I was having no fun in New York, and I wasn't making a living. But flight would signify victory to Winchell, and I wouldn't give the bastard the right to say it.

But I *was* soft once. Winchell once slipped something past his lawyers: in his column, the word "schmuque," meaning me, in an item that alluded to something I'd said on the air. One of America's leading attorneys called me at home on a Sunday night (when the item appeared in an early edition) and said, "Barry, the word has only one meaning, and in my opinion, it is grounds to swear out a warrant for his arrest on charges of criminal libel. If you let me go, I'll have Winchell booked and jailed within the hour!" I listened, and said I'd call him back. I called another lawyer to ask his opinion. He advised me against it in a variety of cajoling ways. I decided against pressing charges. Later I found that the attorney who had talked me out of it had represented Winchell in other actions. I thought about an action against him at the Bar Association, but it would have been pointless. The man, though his name was still on the door of his law firm, was inactive, and suffering senility, his days of advocacy practically over.

There is one person who must be singled out here for bravery in combat. Steve Allen. He was advised that

"Winchell wouldn't like it if you went on the air with Barry." Steve replied, "I wouldn't like myself if I didn't."

But as is said, "God, in his infinite wisdom." Winchell failed on television. Sullivan got more powerful. Winchell's ravings lost him paper after paper, and finally the great *Daily Mirror* folded. He was now a man without a public. He talked about his new passion—golf—while walking about, carrying a putter on the city's streets. He talked, and talked, and talked. His wife died. His son died, under suspicious circumstances. And Winchell was sued by his daughter-in-law for support for herself and their small family. And finally Winchell died. He had barely a quorum at his funeral. Of the millions who read him, of the thousands who served him, of the clan who did his bidding, his only real mourner was his daughter. He received large obituary notices; and finally, a lifetime of evil and spying had ended.

His had been the chance for true greatness. For until Franklin D. Roosevelt died, Winchell had seemed like the white hope of the Fourth Estate. And then Harry Truman came to power, and he despised Winchell and the way he wrote. It seemed to Truman like peeking through the bedroom and bathroom windows. And Winchell went berserk. He was rebuffed by Eisenhower, used by Joe McCarthy, and then went totally conservative politically. He died a failure. Oh, he was a failure, or else you could remember something he said or wrote. What really was his coup de grâce, and for all other columnists as well, was the arrival of Jack Paar on the nightly television scene. He took news columns and read them aloud, with appropriate, humorous comments that made them, and particularly Winchell's, ridiculous. Winchell attempted retaliation. But he forgot his own advice to others. Paar "went to press" as often, in many more cities, and with a much larger audience than Winchell's readership. Winchell's own philosophy, "Don't fight with me, I go to press too often!" had caught up with him and laid his sad, bitter career to rest.

Winchell, Sullivan, Runyon, the Stork Club, Dorothy and Dick, Lindy's, etcetera, were all a far cry from Red Lion, New Jersey, where I was born. Want to find it on the map? Forget it! It doesn't even rate a "wide spot in the road" description. It was actually a dairy farm, near New Brunswick, New Jersey, run by a family named Miranov, with whom my parents, Manuis and Dora Yaroslaw, had become friendly. And while I was getting a prenatal free ride, an epidemic hit the Middle Atlantic States in 1916. My mother, hiding out from the bugs, decided to give birth on the Miranov farm.

I was then brought back to Atlantic City, where my father was the assistant superintendent of the local Metropolitan Life Insurance Company office. A long way from his beginnings: getting off the boat in 1906 from Genoa, Italy (a way stop from Odessa, Russia), without a word of English at his command. But he was strong, young, single, and good-looking, trying his luck at peddling pots and pans from door to door. How you do this without language facility is beyond me, and he never explained it to my satisfaction, but after a variety of jobs, he knew enough English to get a job with Metropolitan as an agent, and one night my uncle took him home for dinner. And that's how he met my mother, and our clan began to take shape. My older brother and sister, then me, and finally, my youngest sister.

My father, prospering between insurance and real estate, felt that Atlantic City was too small for his high-rolling talent and decided to move us all to Los Angeles.

That's a trip the railroad is still trying to find us for. He bought a drawing room and put the whole mob on board. My brother, then 13, and *big*, didn't qualify for a half-fare ticket, so each time the conductor came around to check on the occupants of the drawing room (my infant sister rode free), my brother was in the john. The conductor could only reach the conclusion that my brother had been seriously poisoned by railroad food and had taken a long-lasting cathartic, or had been flushed to the tracks by the downdraft of the old-fashioned plumbing. In the five days it took to ride the train from Atlantic City to Los Angeles, the conductor never saw my brother once!

We arrived in Los Angeles in the early twenties when that city had but 100,000 population. My father parked us all in the railroad station and went out to find an apartment, never thinking (or maybe he did) that an inexpensive hotel might serve for a day or two. He located us near the U.S.C. campus. And proceeded to work again at Metropolitan, only now as a lowly agent, for he had lost his seniority and position in making the move to the West. But he cared little; he was much more interested in the real estate bonanzas that loomed everywhere.

So he bought everything he could. Simply. Little down payment, huge mortgages, and praying that L.A. would grow as quickly as he dreamed. It grew, but about twenty years too late. He lost all the land through lack of tax payment, but his instincts were perfect. Where he'd purchased land, there stand today some of the most impressive corporations in America: Sears, Roebuck; the Bank of America; Thrifty Drug Stores; and Republic Aviation, where once there were empty lots owned by a mad Russian who couldn't hedge his bets. My son, now a NASA officer at Edwards Air Force Base in California, watches aircraft take off each day from land that my father once owned (forty acres of Bartlett pears and two mules and a well)—land that my father lost when tax time came around.

He turned to gambling, and became compulsive. After all, you couldn't manage an insurance debit, real estate, and bets at the same time. And the temptation to use the company's money must have been fierce. He gambled on everything. He would bet you the next fly that flew into the room would have a green eye, and he lost most of his bets. And then, to add to his day, they built Santa Anita Race Track in California, and my father's life was complete. Now he could spend his afternoons where the real action was. A $2 bettor, screaming at the world for the cards it had dealt him.

During the predawn hours he took a small truck he'd purchased, went to the local wholesale produce market, and bought fruits and vegetables; then he made the rounds from small store to small store, selling his wares at a minute markup. The store owners were delighted at the chance to buy their foodstuffs at curbside, rather than getting up early in the morning to do their own shopping. They were too small to have the large truckers call on them. So my father nickeled and dimed his way to Santa Anita every day of the season. And his years went. Edging out a living, sometimes making the rent, sometimes not. Kiting a check here and there, and living on the slim edge of poverty all his remaining days. But he went in style. For he was a stylish man. He read everything. He had strong opinions about everything. And he gained a command of the language that was fantastic. He attended night school with my mother for four years to get his citizenship, and to his dying day his certificate of naturalization was the proudest document in the house.

But about his dying day. He had had a winning day at Santa Anita. He was driving home, and suddenly he collapsed over the wheel and the car edged to a stop. When a passerby opened the door, he was dead. Across the street was a luncheonette. My brother was sitting there, having coffee with a friend in a neighborhood he hadn't been in in years. They noticed a small knot of people gathering outside, and the police arrived. They went to see what was going on, and my brother was the one who identified my father for the police. But what makes it more occult was that they had not spoken for years over some long-forgotten argument. What had brought my father's car to a stop directly opposite that luncheonette?

I was in New York then, working at WMCA, and doing a tape. My producer took a phone call from L.A. while I was on the air. When the show was over, he came in and said, "Barry, I have some bad news for you," and without a moment's hesitation and not knowing why, I said, "My father's dead." My response has bothered me for years. How did I know? What wavelength had brought me the news? I flew to California that night and attended the services the next day. I looked at the stranger in the coffin. Waxen, too much makeup. That wasn't my father. He had been garrulous, happy, outgoing. I'd last seen him when my niece got married and I flew to California for the festivities. It was the first time I said, "C'mon, Pop, let me buy you a drink." And we had sat there like men. I was his crony, his friend, and we were in love with each other.

I returned to New York that funeral night, New Year's Eve, on a flight on which I was the only passenger. And when I arrived in New York and home, the members of my family were asleep in their various rooms. The loss of my father suddenly hit me, and I was torn by sobs. I cried long, and alone, for I knew how high this man had aimed, and how hard he had tried, and how the bastards had ground him down. If he had been born in another time, in my time, he would have been a fantastic success in anything he chose to do. But it was fate that dealt, even to that last winning day, the manner in which he lived and died without ever having had a sick day in his life.

To this day I will reach for the phone to have the weekly chat with him we always enjoyed and suddenly realize he isn't there to answer. If there is immortality in remembrance, he has it, for there has hardly been a day when he hasn't been in my mind. He was one hell of a man, even in the picking of his funeral plot, which he had done a few years before his death. He went to the cemetery where Al Jolson is buried, The Hillside in Los Angeles, and he chose a plot near the golf course and close to the airport highway. And he said, "I like it here —it is 'fralich' [happy]. There they play golf, and over there the cars going by, and here is a bench where once in a while my friends can come and talk to me." That's just the way it played. I have sat on the bench every time I've gone to California, and talked to him.

My mother, who was five years his junior, started to die the day he did. For years she had ragged him about his gambling, his get-rich-quick schemes, his torn-pocket life-style. But when he died she had that vacant look about her. And I wondered what she would be like when the mourners had left, the buffet hounds had departed, and the house was without Joe for the first time. She insisted on living alone, never wanting to live with or burden any of the children. She had a little money. And she obviously wanted to be alone with her thoughts and memories. But one night she suffered a minor stroke, and at her insistence, she was placed in a nursing home, where she lingered.

It was the middle of a week, and my wife said, "Why don't you go out to L.A. this weekend and see your mother?" I asked, "Why this weekend?" And she said, "I don't know." I went to California that Saturday and saw my mother in the nursing home on Saturday afternoon. She had been moved to a larger, beautifully furnished room, facing a patio. And she kept saying, "I wonder why they put me in this beautiful room." And then in a minute or two, "It takes so long to die."

I saw her that day and the next, and flew home on Sunday. The ravages of bed rest had taken their toll of this strong woman who had worked hard all her life trying to make do on pennies, and she wanted to die. Really wanted it. I got home Monday morning, and on Tuesday she died, and I was on my way back to California. I now knew why they had put her in the big and overly spacious room. It was their "dying" room. I spoke to an analyst friend of mine years later about my wife's suggestion and my sudden urge to see her that weekend, and her death immediately thereafter. He told me, "She had finished her business. If you had not gone to California for another month, she would have lived. But you arrived, her only child away from the nest—and there wasn't anything left to live for. She just picked up the chips and left the game."

How many memories crowd in on me as I write! Our frequent movings because of nonpayment of rent, and finally a tiny house in West Los Angeles, where my life changed, because the schools had changed. I transferred from Hollenbeck Junior High School, populated in the main by youngsters of Mexican ancestry, blacks, and poor whites, to Mount Vernon Junior High School, on the other side of Los Angeles, then an all-white school, with all white teachers, and all-white quality education. I was too young to realize it at the time, but where I'd come from the teachers gave the students a halfhearted stab at education, at keeping them busy. They had "given up on them" by the time the students were 10 or 11. At Mount Vernon you were given arduous, painstaking classroom work, personal attention, and *homework*.

Needless to say, my grades, my work, and my feeling about school changed drastically. I began to enjoy it. Where at Hollenbeck the trick was just to get through the day and get out onto the playground, where you tried to avoid fights (even then there were knives), things were very different at Mount Vernon. One was required to wear shirt and tie to school, sit up straight, listen, learn, and recite. And my father wasn't interested in C's and D's. He wanted to see top grades, and in addition, suggested—no, demanded—that I attend Hebrew school, "cheder," after school each day, for the period of my confirmation, "Bar Mitzvah," was approaching.

When we lived on the east side in the Hollenbeck area, going to cheder was like walking the plank every day. For it took me on a three-mile route through neighborhoods that reeked of anti-Semitism, and you had to run, or fight. I became an expert "track and field man" during that period. But as my thirteenth birthday approached, my parents decided, notwithstanding my four years of Hebrew learning, to forgo the ceremony, and I was all for it because I was a terrible Talmudic scholar; they had found that even the simple repast and ceremony were beyond our means. To this day when I tell the story to a friendly rabbi, he volunteers to perform the ceremony, but I'm afraid that I'm far beyond the pale, and I don't need the Bar Mitzvah to be reminded of my faith. My mail reminds me every day, whenever there is a controversy brewing, only my vitriolic mail uses street euphemisms for Jew. By now I've heard them all.

But Mount Vernon's educational attitude has remained with me throughout my life. For there was never a better example for me of the dual standard that governs the education accorded the underprivileged and those whom the teachers *think* there is a chance for. If only they poured that effort into every child, what a different world this might be! Rather than take for granted the genetic lie that "minority, poor kids just can't make it, so why try?" Oh, we were poor, but through the happenstance of school boundaries, I just squeezed over into the good-school area. But the teachers didn't know that. To them I was just another face, eager for learning.

Poor? I remember the graduation exercises in June of the year. Our class colors were orchid and white. The class voted to have the young ladies graduate in white dresses of summer weight of their choosing. The young men were to wear navy blazers, white flannel slacks, and orchid neckties against a white shirt. The necktie cost, with matching kerchief for the breast pocket, $1.50. The flannel slacks were $5. I worked practically the whole term at every odd job—cutting lawns, running errands, passing out handbills—in an effort to come up with the money. When I did graduate, I had the tie, kerchief, and slacks, but I had to borrow the blue jacket. And then on to Los Angeles High School, which in those days was like saying you were going to Harvard or Yale. It was a school heavily weighted in academics. It was a beautiful structure; it had the first high school swimming pool in America. Its teams were outstanding, and you literally could form the foundation of your life at L.A. High. Its graduates were welcomed in the Ivy League colleges, at U.S.C., and at Stanford. In those days, U.C.L.A. didn't count. I majored in history and English, and my English teacher changed my life.

She was a Miss Katherine Carr, and her brother was the leading columnist on the *Los Angeles Times*—the big paper in town. One day, after class, she stopped me and asked what I intended to do when I graduated (I was then a tenth-grade freshman). I said I had no idea. She said, "Why don't you think of writing? Your compositions seem to have a flair."

That was all I needed. Praise from Caesar indeed! I immediately applied for a reporter's spot on the school's daily, then the only high school daily in the country. Accepted, I haunted the *L.A. Times* and the *Examiner* (the Hearst paper) just to watch the metropolitan dailies in action. I took typing courses and learned the touch system. I went to night school and studied linotyping, for I thought a "newspaperman" should know how a paper is put together. My journalism career was blooming while the rest of my grades were terrible.

I also tried out for the Class C football team. I weighed about 90 pounds then, and was about 5 feet tall. You qualified for "C" football by weighing under 110. The trick used by aspirants was to diet until weighing at season's beginning, and then afterward, eating normally, climb to about 125 or even 135. I didn't have to diet. I weighed 90.

My career ended quickly. In a tryout scrimmage, from the position of left end, I attempted to block a field goal. The opposition kicker's ball went over my head. His cleated shoe didn't. There went my dreams of wearing the heavy cardigan sweater with a huge L.A. on it. Well, hell, I could still cover the games. And cover them I did. I was the biggest pain-in-the-ass on campus. I wrote football stories, locker-room anecdotes, gossip gleaned in the halls, and did everything but follow the school hooker home to get her financial status.

By the time I reached the senior year at L.A. High, all classes but journalism and English had palled. I was 15, and had discovered the delights of Main Street (skid row), where five times a day one could observe the nubile delights of gyrating, bumping, grinding, and sensuous-looking females. I'd watch and see the marvelous comics of burlesque as they performed in such routines as "Pay the Two Dollars," "Floogle Street," and "Who's on First?"

By skipping lunch and thumbing rides, I could make the admission price; by skipping classes, I could make the performance. So whenever the bill changed, and sometimes before it did, I would check into school, attend a class or two, write some copy for the *Blue and White* daily, and scurry as fast as my thumb could take me to the "Follies," where all the action was, at 4th and Main Streets. It was a typical burlesque house of the period. There were the comics; the girls; the tenor who sang as the girls "changed," or got ready for a solo undress number; and the hawker in the aisle who sold chocolate-covered peanuts and gimcracks between numbers. I was in the balcony (all I could afford)—enchanted, laughing, and horny!

My idyllic arrangement went on for some weeks—school, Follies, school, home—until one day there was a tap on my shoulder, and as I looked up, I saw a man with "Fuzz" written all over him. He asked, "Where do ya go to school, son?" I told him. He said, "Come with me." Within the hour I was back at L.A. High looking into the eyes of the counselor, who after a brief hearing gave me 30 demerits for truancy. That wouldn't mean anything unless you understood the school's merit system. You started off your school year with 100 merits, and for each infraction you lost 1 or 2, until you scraped bottom at 70, at which point you failed what was euphemistically called "citizenship." That automatically put you back into a lower grade for one year, and what it meant to me was that I could not graduate with my class in June. I went home scared and told my story. I was immediately pronounced a "bum." *But*—there was a ray of sunshine.

My brother, months before, had enlisted in the Civilian Conservation Corps. It was established by President Roosevelt to employ jobless young men and send them off to chop trees, build roads, etcetera, throughout the country, and they received $30 per month, of which $25 was sent home and $5 given to the inmate. Yes, inmate. But since my brother's enlistment, he had found work. So I went in his name. A little small for the description of him, a lot weaker physically, but there were hundreds of us, and who cared? What really bothered me, and for weeks, was getting used to answering to his name.

We were sent via day coach to a place called Challenge, California. I dare you to find it on the map. It lies northeast of Sacramento, near the Nevada line, and the *big* cities nearby are Oroville and Yuba City. They were villages in the early thirties before the freeways, the population explosion of World War II, and the postwar period, and they were our Saturday-night whoop-de-do towns.

From early Monday morning until Saturday afternoon, we chopped trees—and I don't mean with power saws, either. We were commanded by Army officers. Breakfast was at 5:30, and simple fare it was. It made the Army food of later years seem like New York's Plaza. Lunch was two sandwiches, always one of baloney and one of jam, and something to drink. There was an early dinner, and then sack time in double-deck bunks. During the workday, when you wanted a rest stop, you just walked into the thick woods to relieve yourself. One day, in so doing, I dropped my pants and shorts, and almost squatted on a coiling rattler. I recall being constipated for a week.

Your term of service in the CCC was six months unless you got a letter from an employer who had a job for you. I wrote a pleading letter to my family to "bust me out." The neighborhood butcher sent a letter hiring me. I will never forget that train ride back to civilized Los Angeles, going through Sacramento, down the inland route, and by the time we left Bakersfield I could have walked the last 100 miles to L.A.

I remember those "great" bacchanals in Oroville, where fifteen of us would arrive on a Saturday night on the back of an Army truck for a dance being held in town. We would pile off the truck, first arranging to meet the vehicle again at midnight, and move on to the dance. From somewhere a pint of "Pure Panther" would appear, guaranteed aged a week. A few of those and you'd dance with anyone.

Sooner or later, her town date and a couple of friends would wait for you to take some air. The next thing you knew, you were being helped into the truck and were being told, "Boy, what a great time you had!" Or "You were doin' real good till that rangy bastard caught you under the eye. I think he was wearin' brass knucks!" No matter. You had been to town, drunk too much, danced with a pretty girl; the lumps would disappear, and for months, even years, to come you'd think about that Harvest Moon dance in Oroville. The rest—blackout. Like doing time. I didn't eat another baloney sandwich until the Army insisted on it, and to this day it is on my distaste list.

My butcher career started. It was a kosher shop, so I worked Sunday through Friday afternoon, with Friday night and Saturday off. Salary, $8 weekly. I gave $5 to Ma. On the remaining $3 I started compulsively what has never left me, the buying habit. I saved for a $10 pair of shoes. Ten dollars? Then? For a butcher boy? I saved for a $40 custom-made suit. Forty dollars? In the thirties? But I wanted to audition for local radio stations, not to mention going out with girls.

What it worked out to was hustling my ass making deliveries of flanken, roasts, and chops from early morning until late afternoon, and using the butcher's phone to call radio stations between deliveries asking (in the most baritone voice possible) for the chief announcer, a breed that existed in those days. When I managed to get through the secretary, and actually got the man on the horn, I made my pitch, giving him out-of-state references, because I figured they took longer to check, and asked for an audition. At night I would practice reading aloud from magazine ads for cigarettes, soap, shoes, etcetera, in an effort to improve diction, enunciation, delivery.

I managed to wangle two auditions. One was at the local CBS station, where the chief, one Don Forbes, suffered through my nervous, strident, high-pitched reading. And then, afterward, he told me, "You need more experience for CBS. You have something [whatever it was, he wasn't buying it], but come and see us again at some future date. And remember, when you're on the air, don't yell at an audience. Talk, calmly, to one person." It was the best advice I ever received.

I used it at the next audition. Dropping my sights, I applied to an independent local station, KMTR. It operated out of a converted residence just above Hollywood Boulevard. I read for the chief, Rudy Cornell, after having told him I'd worked in Atlanta, Georgia. I got the job. At $125 per month! An absolute fortune then! I worked six days a week, announcing religious programs, writing copy, playing records, working as an engineer in the record stints, and on Sunday I was honored to announce a live program with four lady musicians who called themselves the "Cowbelles." The instrumentation? A cello, two fiddles, and a guitar. They were sponsored at 4 in the afternoon by a man named Mundy, who made hair oil. And so he called the group "Mundy's Cowbelles."

One Sunday I had worked the usual morning shift, opening the station at 6, and running the gamut of assignments—religious hustlers, records, news, commercials, etcetera—and gone home to grab a nap before returning to do the Mundy program. I was still living at home, miles from the studio, and at 3:15 my mother shook me and asked, "Aren't you doing a program at four?" I woke in shock. Threw my clothes on. Dashed into the car (a Chevvy I'd bought for $12), and with the accelerator on the floor, I roared through the streets at 20 miles per hour. I arrived at KMTR a blink before 4. Just as the red light went on over the studio door and Mundy was on the air. I ran to the microphone as the flurry of introductory theme chords was played by the young ladies, and yelled, "From Hollywood, we bring you Mundy's Cowballs!—*belles!*" The studio chose to overlook the gaffe. But I should have read some more of those ads from the magazines at home, and tried to be earlier.

I must go back a moment. During my butcher-boy days, my brother, now and for years a studio electrician, ran sound trucks in Southern California towns at supermarket openings and world premieres, and sometimes he would put up one klieg light for a cigar store's first night. It is hard for those outside of the L.A. area to understand the phenomenon of the time, but garishness was *in* then. And no one thought it garish—it was just the California way of doing things. If you opened a new supermarket, you sent a sound truck through the streets, with a driver, doubling as announcer, hawking your opening, the special prices, and the location, with the date of opening. Then, on opening day, or days, you provided a large, wheeled stage in front of the supermarket, and with streamers flying, searchlights crossing the sky, you presented a full-scale show. An orchestra, singer, dancers, comics, and an emcee.

My brother was in this business and was easily the best emcee entrepreneur in the field, while I was merely a butcher boy, but he allowed me to ride in the sound truck through an L.A. neighborhood and make the announcements required. I thought I would die of mike fright, hearing my voice amplified all over the community. That was the first time. Within three months you couldn't have kept me away from it. The ham in me had flowered. But lights and fury to signify an opening were a fad, and the fad perished. My passion for broadcasting didn't, however. And from KMTR on, I was an addict.

The job lasted six months. I could give you a million

theories on why I was fired. But the simple reason? The owner, the late Victor Dalton, didn't like me—or my work.

The day I was dropped, an announcer named Carl Bailey called me. He was leaving a midnight–until–6 A.M. job on KGFJ, sponsored by a local clothing store, the Victor Clothing Company. The program originated from the transmitter directly across from a funeral parlor in midtown L.A. The job consisted of spinning records all night long, with five two-minute commercials an hour. And patter was expected before each record! It did pay $125 per month, but no days off.

I would arrive at the studio; let myself in; climb six flights; sign in; and say good evening to the engineer, who promptly went to sleep; and then I talked to myself all night, for I was sure no one was listening. Save one. That was the sponsor, who would call me at 5 in the morning to tell me that I had not "punched" that last commercial enough.

His was a shlock operation whose clientele was mainly Filipinos. They loved clothes, and holding menial jobs, they bought them on credit. Victor Clothing offered them a *complete* outfit for $22.50. By complete, I mean shoes, socks, garters, suit, shirt, hat, and cuff links. If you wanted an overcoat, it was $5 more, but no one did. His customers *believed* that California was always warm. For each month that I had 50 people visit the clothing company as a result of my commercials, I got an outfit free. I had the job 16 months before I quit. I owned 16 outfits, including a riding habit (and I didn't ride then). I quit because I was getting buggy with the commercials, the funeral parlor across the way which rolled its garage doors up about six times a night to go pick up a newly deceased customer, the sleeping engineer, and finally, the "Where is this job gonna take me?" syndrome.

I had saved a few hundred dollars, and for months had mulled over the idea of going to New York to try my fortune. It was clinched by the "open auditions" which were held infrequently by L.A. stations to find an announcer to sell a particular product on a weekly or daily program. I attended them all. And time after time, after all the local voices were heard, they would say that they were bringing in someone from New York to do the show. It occurred to me that if I played my cards right and went to New York, I might, one day, be the guy *from* New York they were bringing in. In 28 years, it has happened three times. Some average!

I made the trip by train, sitting up in the day coach, and it took five days. I was met at Grand Central by a friend who had lived in Los Angeles and had moved to the Bronx, near the then fashionable Grand Concourse Plaza. He and his family invited me to be their houseguest while I looked for a job in New York and got settled. What bravado I had then! I thought it was merely a question of announcing, "I am here!" and job offers would come flying in.

I had met Bert Parks in Los Angeles, when he was there as singing announcer with the Eddie Cantor show, and he'd said, "Look me up when you come to New York." To me that was as good as an offer to come to work at CBS, where Bert was on staff—and I would add, that was the finest staff of announcers ever assembled in American radio. I promptly visited CBS in Manhattan, and I haunted its studios for four days. Bert was out; Bert was tied up; Bert was on the air; Bert couldn't see me today—I believed it all. Then one day I saw him on the street outside CBS and asked if he could advise me on job opportunities. He shrugged and said, "I don't see how." And he moved away—smartly. I felt like such a shmuck!

And now I began to make the rounds of all the Manhattan radio stations. No jobs anywhere. Certainly none for a guy from out of town with vague references from the boondocks—that's what L.A. was in those days. I continued to live in the Bronx with my friends, and off of them, and used up what money I had. I haunted radio stations, wore out shoe leather, and learned the subway routes perfectly. I was now down to no money, but had an extensive Victor Clothing Company wardrobe. So I started to sell suits, riding boots, tuxedo to the friendly pawnbroker in the neighborhood. The going rate for the suits in perfect condition was $10. I finally ran through my wardrobe, except what I had on my back. When I was down to my typewriter, I sold that. Finally the return on that dwindled to the point where, as I trudged down Broadway past the site of today's Bond Clothing Store in Times Square, I had, in my pocket, a dime. That was it. The price of a candy bar, and the then nickel subway fare back to the Bronx. I looked up, and there was the marquee of Broadway's newest and flossiest nightclub, the International Casino, starring Milton Berle and featuring Diosa Costello in her dance.

Back in L.A. I had met Milton's brother, Jack, who was a salesman for Victor Clothing. I had nothing to lose. I was near starvation, and broke. It was early evening and Berle might be in. I walked up the great, golden stairs of the club. Entering, I asked the captain, poring over his reservation book, if Mr. Berle was in. I gave my name, and added, "I'm a friend of his brother's in Los Angeles."

In a moment or two, a tall, distinguished-looking gray-haired lady came out and announced herself as Milton's mother. She took me into Milton's dressing room. He was lounging in a chair and shooting glances at himself in the makeup mirror.

He gave me a quick look and said, "Siddown, kid." He asked me about Jack. That took fifteen seconds. He asked me what I'd been doing in New York. That took a minute. He then asked me, "Do ya need any money?" I thought I'd cry. I said, "Yes, I'm broke." He reached into his pocket and peeled off three $10 bills. He said to his mother, "Take him out front for the show and dinner."

Show and *dinner*? I hadn't eaten that whole day. We walked into the golden, fantastic world of New York's most beautiful club, and were ushered to the best seats in the place. Mama Berle ("Call me Sadie") ordered soup for me, and steak, and vegetables, and dessert, and coffee. She *was* the embodiment of the Jewish Mother. She kept asking, "Do you like it?" I had difficulty answering. I was too busy chewing and swallowing.

Then came the show, and I was mesmerized. The gorgeous line of girls, the backdrop—the most beautiful stage ever, the full orchestra, and 18-year-old Diosa Costello! What a face, what a figure, and what a dancer. She wriggled, writhed, moved, and shimmied, and tiny as she was, she filled the stage with her presence. And then, finally, the star was announced, Milton Berle. On our table were two tiny wooden hammers, used to applaud the acts, and Mama Berle handed me one and said, "Hammer! Hammer!"

Filled with high protein, I thought I'd break the table with my enthusiasm. Berle was great. Truly great. He dominated the stage then, as he does now. Since then,

I've heard his jokes a thousand times. He never fails to make me laugh. He has been described many ways. To me he is deep, feeling, compassionate, and sensitive; and since that first meeting he has become my friend, and a man I admire intensely. The stories of his manifold giving are rarely, if ever, told. But many of those who get great press for their "giving" couldn't equal his record for humanitarianism if they had started 100 years ago. Just ask any performer.

After the show, we went back to Berle's dressing room, and as he toweled off he said, "I'll make a call for you tomorrow, and see if I can get you an audition." He did call. WMCA was putting on summer help for the World's Fair. It needed a couple of announcers. I was auditioned and hired. Forty dollars per week! It was one of the happiest days of my life, except that I was a morning man again. I had to open the station at 7, and my Bronx friends were moving to Brooklyn, the Bay 34th Street area. I moved with them, and for $10 per week got room and dinner. I had to get up at 5 if I was to get to work barely on time. But I was in New York radio! For six months, and then the cutback came.

So by now I knew for sure I needed more stuff to cut the New York mustard, and I headed home, via Chicago. I stayed there too long. I used too much of what little money I had. It came November, and I had no coat. I started to hitchhike—from Chicago to Kankakee, from Kankakee to Springfield—and then it started to snow. I couldn't afford meals *and* a room. I asked at the YMCA if I could sleep in the empty, warm ballroom. I was turned away. A temple took me in for the night, but first I sent a wire, collect, to my brother in L.A. asking for bus fare home. The bus left the next day at 1 P.M. The money arrived at noon. I ran to the station, boarded the bus, and got home five days later. Well, I had seen America! I paid my brother back, $1 a week, when I had it. And Berle, too, finally got back his $30. But I'll never stop paying the interest on that loan, in telling of the night at the International Casino.

In L.A. I started the audition route again. No jobs. But an NBC executive, Buddy Twiss, hearing me at an audition, called to ask if I would be interested in an announcing job at the network's station in Salt Lake City, KDYL. Salary, $125 a month. I grabbed it, and was on a bus for Salt Lake the next day, having hurriedly packed and picked up a book called *Children of God*—required reading for all those wishing to inhabit the home of the Latter-day Saints. On the bus, en route, I read of the church's leader, Joseph Smith, killed by a mob at Nauvoo, Illinois. How the Mormons, seeking a new home, made their way westward and after long, arduous, and dangerous travel, with their new leader, Brigham Young, dying in the back of a covered wagon, they were able to describe to him the Great Salt Lake Basin. He then uttered those now immortal words, "This is the place." And Salt Lake City, a barren desert, salt-encrusted, is today the green oasis of the Wasatch Mountain area.

It's a beautiful city, with the finest church architecture in America. The Mormon Temple was built entirely by hand and has not even one nail in its structure. It dominates the center of the city, with a statue of Young standing in front. The Mormon-run bank faces it across the street. On its left is the Mormon-run Hotel Utah, and across the street from it the Mormon-run department store—reputedly the first department store in America. Of the statue, natives crack, "There he [Young] stands, with his ass to the church and his hand toward the bank."

The Mormons are a remarkable people, as I came to find out. They tithe their working members, assessing them a portion of their earnings each year to take care of their poor. They accepted no Federal aid during the Great Depression. Their young men and women undertake missionary work throughout the world before they pick up the threads of their adult lives, and everyone except a Mormon is termed a "Gentile" in Latter-day Saints' country. They have a unique, salty humor about them.

I was again a station-opener at KDYL. And each day, as I walked to work at sunrise, the early rays would catch, brilliantly, the golden statue of Moroni, the Mormons' guardian angel, as he stood on the highest spire of the temple. From time to time, steeplejacks would be called in to sandblast the temple clean. Two were once summoned from Los Angeles for a job estimate. They were asked, after they'd inspected the job, what it would cost. When told the price, the church president said, "That's pretty high, isn't it?" And the non-Mormon steeplejacks replied, "Yeah—but this is a dirty bastard of a job!"

The Mormons, having been decimated by mob violence that killed off many of their men, had practiced polygamy as a protective way of life for their women. Each Mormon was required to take as many wives as he could afford. Brigham Young had the most. The reported figure is 21. In the 1930's, a film company made a movie of his life, and the studio heads decided to premiere it in Salt Lake City. They also decided to bring the Young descendants to town for the world opening. The main street was filled with buses, all carrrying the Young progeny. It was quite a tribute to his diet. Not to mention his rod and staff.

I didn't tarry in Salt Lake City. It was too quiet for

a city fella, and I wanted to get back to L.A. and try again. I landed a part-time, which turned into a full-time, job at KMPC in Beverly Hills. Its studios were then on Wilshire Boulevard about a block west of the Beverly-Wilshire Hotel. The station carried some programs from CBS, and it was certainly considered a class operation. It originated programs, wrote its own news, carried remotes, and if nothing else, had the flossiest address in town, even though a gas station was next door.

Selective service had been enacted while I was in Salt Lake City. I had registered, of course, and notified my draft board of my new address. The Hollywood grapevine had it that if you enlisted in the service through the Motion Picture Academy of Arts and Sciences and were found qualified, you would be assigned to making motion-picture training films at the Signal Corps laboratories in Astoria, Long Island, New York. The local office was on Vine Street, near Hollywood Boulevard. I went down and asked for an interview, which was granted, and was qualified as a writer. I applied for enlistment, and was called for a physical in July, 1941. The Army was so persnickety then that I was turned down for being 5 pounds underweight for my height. I was now 6 feet 3 inches tall, and weighed about 145. I was told to go home, drink a lot of water, and eat bananas. This I did. I was called for another physical, and I passed. And I figured, Why not? I was 1A. I was sure to be called. Better writing training films than slogging through a ditch somewhere in Georgia. I was summoned for induction on December 5, 1941—beating the Japanese to the war by two days!

On induction day there were hundreds of us lounging about the induction center from early morning until about 5 P.M. Questionnaires, final-type physical, "Do you like girls?," swearing-in. And then, onto buses which took us to Fort MacArthur, California, an artillery base, for a sandwich dinner and our first night in the barracks. The next morning, issuance of uniforms, listening to the Articles of War, and finally a pass to go home until the next day—Sunday, December 7—to show the home folks their "soldier." I was beautiful. My uniform fitted me as if I'd been measured in a Mixmaster. I also smelled of mothballs. And the Army shoes had a distinct yellow cast. But the hell with that! I was off to write scenarios for training films, *and* in New York. And a *real* chance to see the Big Apple.

I awoke Sunday, late, to learn of Pearl Harbor. Radio voices shrilled out that all military personnel must return to their bases at once. I went, and will never forget the scene in the rail depot. My family carried on as though I were shipping out for the outer islands of Japan that night! But I knew different. *I* was going to be making films. I got back to the fort and was assigned to a tent. Inside were my "comrades in arms" who were also tagged for the film center in Astoria. Jackie Searle, the "boy" actor; Lawrence Tibbett, Jr., son of the great operatic baritone; and a writer from MGM, Jerry Kurtz. It was raining, as it can rain only in California, where it never rains. And through the torrent and past the thrown-aside tent flap came a sergeant who stuck his head in to announce, "You pricks can forget about making movies. You're in the Army now!"

The next day I was assigned as a teletype operator in a Signal Corps outfit. I subsequently fought the Battle of the "Top of the Mark" in San Francisco for seven months. Then I moved my command post to Fort Monmouth, New Jersey; then I was transferred to March

Field, California, attached to the Air Corps; then Santa Barbara, California; and finally, Hammer Field, in Fresno, California. You should see my combat ribbons! I flew in tow-target missions, I worked in maintenance squadrons, and I saw a lot of America. But my combat experience was confined to an argument with a sergeant (I was now a corporal) over whose Coke came out of the PX machine first. He won. How can you argue with an extra stripe?

But I experienced a terrible loss during the war. I had become very friendly with Jerry Kurtz, the kid from MGM. We got to know each other well during our brief encounter at Fort MacArthur, and later at Fort Monmouth. He was then commissioned, and went overseas to the European campaigns. He served with valor, and his tunic decorations looked like a Christmas tree. He came home to San Francisco, after his Army discharge, to see his family before returning to work at MGM. He was killed by a drunk driver who ran his car up onto the sidewalk and nailed the walking Jerry.

I was mustered out on a Friday, and with separation pay, my last month's pay, travel pay, etcetera, I was rich! I had about $300. The Army discharged me in West Los Angeles, and gave me 15 cents in travel pay because that was what it would cost to get to my home by city bus. But my mind was made up. I could go back to KMPC, for the President had guaranteed our jobs when we got home. But I had that New York itch again. I'd seen the city again while at Fort Monmouth, and it was the Big Apple. What a city! How I longed truly to be part of it!

And so, on Saturday night, one night out of the Army, I took the Santa Fe Scout for $41 (military rate; I was allowed to wear the uniform for thirty days), and for five days I rumbled across America until I could finally kiss the floor at Grand Central. With barracks bag, I checked around, and registered at the Shelton Hotel. Nine dollars a week then! And with a swimming pool!

My first night in town, I was stopped by two MP's on the corner of 49th and Lexington, in front of the Shelton. "Got a pass, soldier?" "No." "Well, ya got a furlough?" "No." "Whattaya got?" And I opened my blouse pocket to show them my discharge papers. They read them, and muttered, "Lucky bastard!" and walked away.

The next afternoon I walked over to WOR-Mutual at 40th and Broadway to say hello to an old friend, and while we talked I was introduced to the chief announcer. He noted the uniform and asked, "Where are you stationed?" I replied, "I'm not—I've just been discharged." He asked, "Were you in radio?" I told him of KMPC, WMCA, and so forth. He then used the magic words: "Would you like to read for me?" I nodded quickly. We walked into an empty studio. He scared up an engineer, I read, I was hired, and an hour later, in uniform, I was announcing *Chick Carter, Boy Detective*, starring Leon Janney, to the entire Mutual network! I *was* in New York radio!

Well, now the interim stuff has been recorded—and here we are in the early fifties, and I'm in the studios of WMCA, three floors over Lindy's at 51st and Broadway. There is a studio audience each night. We have, out of necessity, started to invite guests, and it is a new ball game. I avoid attendance at Lindy's, although I have a great affection for Leo Lindemann, the owner—but then, he is rarely there when I get off the air anyway, and I don't intend to "walk the plank" nightly.

I had been a member of the Friars Club, a fraternal organization of theatrical personalities. Ed Sullivan is now the Abbot, or headman. I resign when I find that most of the membership fritter away their time, between frolics and card playing, in discussions of the "Winchell–Gray" feud. Many of my fraternal "brothers" are siding with Winchell (who is not a member), and I can see no reason for the privilege of being rapped and paying dues for it.

I resolve, with Nathan Straus, the president of WMCA, that the trick is to keep the show alive and on the air. But the mind plays tricks, and holds memories, and there are hundreds of other days when the world of Broadway was young, and naive, and fun-loving, and one big lark from dusk till dawn. Or was that my description —and in fact was it always sleazy, hard, fast at the jugular, and unrelenting? I know I liked my Broadway then.

I recall the earliest days, the days when the WOR program was just beginning to make its move, and people were starting to stay up late to hear Carol Bruce and the legion of guests who followed her, and my wife was expecting our first child. She had been rushed to the hospital in the seventh month of her pregnancy, and after she'd been bedded down for the night, with the doctor not sure of a delivery or not, I went to the studios, leaving instructions at the hospital that I was to be called at once if anything happened. I sweated the night away, with no word, and made fun of the records, joked with guests, and it was finally 5:45 A.M., and time to go back to the hospital. My wife was in active labor, and I paced the sidewalk at dawn just outside the hospital. Finally, at 7 in the morning, our daughter, Melodie, arrived prematurely, weighing 4 pounds.

It had been "touch and go." Reassured that our baby

would receive the best of care, I went back to our tiny hotel flat to grab a couple of hours of sleep. Then back to the hospital. The doctor informed me gravely that she had contracted "newborn diarrhea," then prevalent in the United States—apparently brought over by war brides. Already that day one infant had died. The nursery was quarantined, and Melodie, if she was to win the fight for her life, would have to be moved. With the doctor, I stood looking at the tiniest human I'd ever seen, who every few moments would contract her body and emit a greenish fluid. Time was of the essence. I asked the doctor what to do. He said, "We'll take her to Mount Sinai" —then, in a soft, kindly tone, "It'll be expensive." I asked, "What's the alternative?" He replied, "Bellevue— where she'll die!"

We wrapped her warmly and took her to the admissions desk at Sinai. As she lay in the basket in the admissions hallway, and the doctor was explaining the emergency, the cashier asked, "How much of a deposit does the father want to make now?" I wrote her a check for $150. I was not sure I could cover it. She was taken upstairs and put into an incubator and given great care and intravenous feeding.

My wife still didn't know of the events of the evening, but lay sleeping in the other hospital where she'd delivered. I went to see her, and lied to her that chances were great for Melodie's recovery—for the doctor had leveled with me, and she barely had a chance. By now she had dropped to 3 pounds 10 ounces. I left the hospital as my wife slept, and went to Lindy's, for I had some hours before I was due to broadcast. Leo took a look at my face and asked me to sit in a back booth and tell him what was going on. I did. We talked for a long time. As I left, he patted my jacket and said, "Don't worry. It'll all work out." That night, as I reached for a cigarette in the pocket that he had patted—the breast pocket, where usually one wears a kerchief—there was Leo's check for $2,000!

Twice each day I visited Melodie, first donning surgical mask and gown, and peered into the glass incubator, where occasionally an eyelid would quiver, showing life. She was being fed intravenously through a tube in her ankle, and she seemed to be holding her own. The fact that she was living from day to day was miraculous. And I reported daily to that other hospital to bring my wife up to date.

While we were speaking on one of those days, I was called by WOR at the hospital. The columnist Leonard Lyons was raising an uproar and wanted to sue me, my guest, and the station. It seems that Ed Weiner, Winchell's man Friday (this was before the feud), had referred, in jest, to Lyons on my broadcast a few nights earlier as the "Antelope Boy of journalism." During that period a newsman had discovered a Tarzan-type youngster in Africa, who he reported could run faster than the speediest beasts of the jungle. It was good for four days of copy, and then it died. Weiner used the analogy because Lyons made it a practice to cover every Broadway spot every night, with great rapidity. But, as I say, the comment was made in jest, not malice. I called Lyons to speak with him to explain the manner in which the comment had been used. He hung up on me. I thought we'd been disconnected. He hung up again. He then wrote a letter to WOR—and later one to WMCA—saying that if I ever mentioned his name again, he would sue! Horseshit! I'll mention his name again. Horseshit!

Years later, when I was talking with the late Joan Carter, she said that Lyons was angry at me for another story. He had heard that I had criticized him, on the air, about dining with Christine Jorgensen. It was untrue. I couldn't have cared less about what he did with Christine Jorgensen—for all I know, it might have helped them both. So I called the Lyons residence—foolishly, I would add, for how many times do you have to ask for the message? "Mrs. Lyons, I've just found out that your husband believes I criticized him for dining with Christine Jorgensen. It isn't true." She said, "There is someone at the door." And hung up. So much for manners at the Lyons house. Some people have told me he's a nice guy.

Beth, my wife, came home, and we continued to visit Melodie twice each day. Miraculously, she was thriving. She was allowed to be moved into the regular nursery, and finally, she came home—at the age of six weeks, and weighing just over 6 pounds! Today she is a beautiful, married young woman, who recently resigned as a fashion editor of *Glamour* to have her first child, and I still kid her about being expensive from the moment she was born. Now let my son-in-law suffer!

Broadway was not all bad guys, or craven characters. It had its noblemen, one of them named Mike Todd. A rough, sometimes uncouth type, but Runyonesque in his heart of gold. We met under unusual circumstances. When I started the all-night show on WOR, I found myself on the opening-night list of the Broadway theaters. It was a great gift. A pair of choice tickets arrived for every opening. You wore black tie to each event. Saw all the "in" people, who mostly looked as though they suffered from chronic constipation; and sometimes you were thrilled, such as when *Death of a Salesman*, *Damn Yankees*, and *South Pacific* came along, and sometimes you were bored beyond belief. As I was on seeing my first Broadway show.

It was Todd's *Up in Central Park*. I thought it awful, God-awful! That night, or morning, at 2 A.M., I went on the air and ranted for half an hour about the theatrical mess I had witnessed. Acting? "Terrible!" Music? "Forgettable!" Reason for being? "None!" WOR's boss got a call the next day. Mr. Michael Todd would desire an audience with that kid who did the review the night before. I was summoned, told to be in Todd's office at the appointed time, and left to tremble. I had heard his reputation as a killer. But it was a lousy show!

Two hours later, I walked into the biggest office I had ever seen. At the end of it was Todd behind his desk. From where I stood, he looked like a framed Mussolini with hair, a huge cigar stuck in his mouth. He growled, "You the kid who did the review on *Central Park* last night?" I nodded. He said, "Business at the box office picked up today. I guess nobody believed it could be as bad as you said it was. I just bought time on your program—and I wantcha to do the same kind of review every night until I tell you stop. And I told WOR to put a hundred-a-week talent fee in it for you. Thanks!"

The interview was over. But for some three months I went on the air nightly and rapped *Up in Central Park*. I had to constantly find extemporaneous ways to say it was lousy. And Mike Todd paid for it. We became good friends. We saw each other in many places in New York and out. I saw him in Las Vegas, and he sure was a high roller.

Once I had arrived at the London airport to return to New York, and started to check my baggage in at the BOAC counter, when I was told that because of a sudden fog, it was doubtful whether any aircraft would be landing or departing for some hours. I was furious. Obviously, I had given up my room at my London hotel.

The city and airport facilities were jammed. And all I could see was sleeping on an airport bench and, worst of all, being too late for the broadcast in New York the next night.

I started to storm at the airline clerk, telling him, "I have to get back to New York!" A voice behind me was heard: "Big deal. So they won't hear your big mouth tomorrow night. Those pearls of wisdom. You'll be a day late, and a day better. And they'll be happier to see ya!" I turned at the first sentence, and it was Todd. Smiling. He said, "C'mon." And he took the major part of the passenger group on that flight to dinner in the airport restaurant. Hours later, we took off for New York, and I *was* at work a day late. There wasn't even a ripple from audience or management. I don't think they knew I'd been away.

Years later, a theatrical organization wanted to honor Todd with a "Man of the Year" dinner in New York. Todd was to fly in from California in the very early morning hours for the dinner that night. Weather conditions were bad in the Southwest. He was advised against using his private jet. But a commercial-jet wait was tricky too, for the airlines couldn't guarantee departure because of dire weather predictions. Todd *had* to get to New York. He forgot his own advice of "You'll be a day late, and a day better." He was killed, and Broadway and Elizabeth Taylor were never quite the same again.

And by now the guest roster at the little studio off Times Square had grown. One night I had Frank Sinatra on the air during the Sinatra heyday at the Paramount, and he was and is a fantastically loyal man to his friends. He is also a fierce hater. He invited me to drop in to the Paramount one night after his last show and go with him to an Italian Society benefit. Without my knowledge, at the end of his performances, which no one has ever equaled, he would plug his friend "Barry Gray, who I hope you'll listen to when you get home tonight. He's on WOR at two in the morning." So much for Leonard Lyons.

I went over to the Paramount to watch Frank's last show that night preparatory to accompanying him and George Evans, his manager, to the Italian blast. Backstage, Frank rushed into a black coat and muffler to keep his perspiring throat warm, and we dashed through the subterranean passages of the Paramount to come up into the side lobby of the theater and go directly into a waiting limousine. But the show was just breaking. The side doors were wide open. Two mounted policemen, alerted to Frank's exit, had backed their mounts' rumps into the doors, and as Frank, George, and I emerged, the horses closed around them to provide safe exit into the car. A woman yelled, "There he is" (meaning Sinatra), and swung her handbag in full stride and exuberance. It caught me behind the ear, and I went down, fuzzy. I recall hearing Frank's voice calling, "The skinny guy's with me." I was lifted like a bale and thrown onto the floor of the car, and we pulled away. This was insanity!

It was also during this early period that I met a lady who was a great belter of songs, Belle Baker. She listened each night, and called one night to invite me to see her at the Latin Quarter, then one of Broadway's biggest clubs. It was run by Lou Walters, whose daughter Barbara is the reason I watch the *Today* show on NBC. Belle, in her dressing room, asked, after the amenities, "Do you have an agent?" I said, "No—what for?" She told me why I needed one: contracts, great things to come, guidance, etcetera.

She introduced me to her agent, Jerry Rosen, late of Hollywood. He signed me, and promptly took me to a shirtmaker and tailor, and thereby ruined my life—for I had thought Bond Clothing was pretty snappy. He then booked me for a two-week engagement as an emcee into the Greenwich Village Inn. That was a club which had a piano team named Johnny and George as regulars, and each two weeks it changed the rest of the bill and booked a girl singer. Her voice didn't matter, but her cleavage did—especially on the high notes! Also on the bill were a comic and an emcee.

Joe Laurie, Jr., was my mentor. He asked about the money. I told him, $750 a week. My God! Weeks before, I'd been getting $59 per week! This was America! Seven hundred and fifty dollars *plus* my all-night salary, the Mike Todd fee, opening nights, and a table at Lindy's! Joe then asked, "What're ya doin' for an act?" I told him, "No act, Joe. I'm the emcee, the pointer. All I have to do is introduce the acts." His words, now immortal, stuck in my head. He said, "Kid, anybody can get on—just throw your hat on, and follow it. Getting off is the trick!" I was cocky, overpaid, and unheeding.

Came opening night. Fifteen minutes before opening, while I was putting on my first pancake makeup, I was told by one of the owners that I would do about forty minutes! Forty minutes of what? The band played my "bow music." With absolutely no material, I walked on, and started to ad lib for about three minutes, to an audience composed of everyone I had ever rapped on WOR. The only friendly face I could find—or rather, form—belonged to Joe Laurie, Jr., standing in the back of the room. I bowed off to introduce a young man "just out of the Army, making his debut in New York tonight

—Joey Bishop!" Joey was the riot I should have been. I went directly to work at WOR, beating the papers to the street, and told the audience how bad I'd been. Incredibly bad, inept, stupid, unfunny, and *in person*.

The engagement lasted three nights. The club paid me off, and Earl Wilson gave me a medal for "honest reviewing" in his column. Jerry Rosen, who'd booked the debacle, promptly sold my contract to Paul Small, who was a big, fat man, but supposedly a dynamo as an agent. I'd worked Small over on the air too—not directly, but through some of *his* acts. He booked me shortly into Loew's State Theater. And this time I *was* the emcee! I pointed at acts, five of 'em, five shows a day, for a week. The film? *The Jolson Story*. I think we broke the house record that week. To this day I tell about the house record, and because I'm a fink, I neglect to tell them what picture was playing!

Jolson? He gave me the outstanding program of my life—and that record still stands. Oh, there have been others with much more press space—but his was the greatest! I had heard the sound track of his new film prior to its release. I had loved Jolson from the time I'd literally been in short pants and passed out theater handbills, or sneaked in, just to see *The Jazz Singer*, the first "talkie." Now I raved, and raved, and raved.

Leo Lindy told Jolson about it in a call to the Coast. Jolson had just been in New York, but he returned, and one night I looked up, and in the control room, behind the engineer, stood Jolson, Lindy, and Harry Akst, the Jolson accompanist. I was dumbstruck and invited them into the studio. A tiny cubicle with three microphones and two telephones. After our greeting, Jolson thanked me for my comments in the past, and then asked,

"Where's the piano? I sing better than I talk!" I replied that in this studio, as he could see, we had no piano, but down the hall there was a giant studio, used for Mutual's music shows, and it would take just a minute to switch over. So briefly we went off the air, and then came on again, from the large studio, with Harry Akst at the piano keyboard, Jolson facing me across a felt-covered desk, and a boom (suspended) microphone between us. He sang for almost three hours! And all by request—from me.

The studio started to fill up, as word filtered through Manhattan that Jolie was on the air, and *singing*. It seemed that every star in town was in the studio that night by 3:30 A.M., and sitting on the floor, for we had no chairs. And people telephoned other people to wake them, and tell them what was going on.

Fortunately, a WOR engineer was at home and had recording equipment. He got the whole thing on acetate (there was no tape then), and miraculously, that moment in musical memorabilia has been saved! We started to issue about a hundred sets at cost—but the Decca people, who owned all rights to the Jolson work, stopped us. But I would venture that that set has been bootlegged ten thousand times, or more. I have the original. It has been on the air three times in about a quarter century. It's as "now" as the night it was made!

But Jolson, Joey Adams, Carol Bruce, Sinatra, Como, Stafford meant little to WOR when the crunch of columnists came. I was told the station had been threatened with a press blackout in the columns, which were oh! so powerful then, if I continued to laugh at their items and show how silly they were. Except for Wilson (a gentle man) and Sullivan (simply a chronicler of the passing scene at that time), the columnists were fanatic in attacks on reputations, incursions into private lives, and gossip, and their stuff had very little connection with the public careers of the people they wrote about. They were pickers of offal. And I was too damned fresh! What I failed to realize or know was something I learned the hard way years later in writing a daily column for the *New York Post*. Franklin Roosevelt said it: "No one has something to say five days a week." And so trash filled the Broadway columns regularly—tidbits from press agents, puffs for free meals from restaurants, plugs for ingenues (for free love—what other reason?). In short, it was a jungle, and in jungle fashion I was kicked out of the trees. And then came Miami Beach, and the Copa.

I didn't find it much different really, except that it was a smaller town, and news traveled even faster. I fought with most of the columnists there too. I had one run-in with a man named Reuben Klein, who published a weekly scandal sheet. He sold ads in his paper. I could never prove that buying an ad prevented a scandalous item, but there was an attempted extortion from a public official in Miami Beach. I commented on it on the air. I was summoned by the grand jury. I was admonished by the judge not to discuss my testimony on the air. I didn't, and explained to the radio audience why I couldn't until the information was released by the grand jury. Klein, in his rag, purported to report what I'd said. I called him a liar.

At about 2:45 in the morning, with fifteen minutes left to go on the air, Klein walked up the dais to my microphone. He was a short, heavy, strong, barrel-chested man, who wore no socks, and untied shoes. He was uninvited, and opened by saying, as he sat down next to me, "Did you call me a liar?" I said, "Just a minute, I want

to introduce you. This is Reuben Klein, publisher of—"
and with that, felt a sting on my cheek: he had slapped
me! As I turned to look at him he was rising, to my left,
and poising himself for a left hook, a knockout punch.

I reacted instinctively and bobbed to the right, his left
sailed past me, and I swung with my right, and in my
hand, without thinking, I was holding a pencil microphone. I belted him—hard. He went backward into the
chair, the chair went over, and he lay on his back, bleed-
ing, with his legs in the air. A knockout. And the station
was off the air, for I had knocked the equipment out
with Reuben. They carried him off the dais and propped
him against a wall to recover, and then he stumbled out
of the club.

Jackie Miles, the comic, rushed to my apartment at
about 4 in the morning to hear my story, and advised
me I must press charges, for otherwise Klein might, and
twist the story. So I did. The trial was held within hours
in the Dade County Courthouse. Klein was found guilty,
fined $25, and given a 30-day sentence in jail—suspended.
The real loss to Klein was his reputation as a street
brawler. It was gone overnight. For he had been belted
out by a stripling, and he and his paper skulked the back
streets from then on. It was one of my greater moments.

Back to New York, and Chandler's restaurant in 1950,
and on WMCA, like MacArthur, I had returned: almost
three years older, perhaps a bit wiser—for in Florida
then, much as in Las Vegas today, the horizons were
larger; the guests came from many different walks of life.
Along with Milton Berle, the Ritz Brothers, and Sophie
Tucker, I had also had the opportunity to talk with
David Dubinsky, Walter Reuther, and Senator Pepper

(who through my support became a private citizen, until he returned to the House of Representatives). Chandler's, however, was where it was at! The action was fun, fantastic; the high that one got just from being on the air with the most exciting people in America kept me awake for hours after the program was over. Many nights, when the doors of the saloon closed at about 3:30, we would have private spreads, with many of the stars in New York having a late steak there. Then they'd fall out on the sidewalk at 5:30 and stumble home.

One night, the late George Brandt, of the Brandt Theater family, came in, and called me aside to tell me that his theater chain, the Subway Circuit—so-called because it was not only off Broadway but off the entire borough —was in difficulty. Its star, Bert Lahr, was acting up. Lahr was playing the lead in *Harvey*, the comedy in which Frank Fay had been a fantastic hit on Broadway. Lahr, getting $1,000 per week, wanted a raise—and this while the theater chain was losing money paying him that sum. Brandt wanted to know if I would step into the part. Why not? Now you *know* how cocky-dumb I was! I was to open in eight days.

I prepared in an empty rehearsal hall on the West Side of Manhattan. I was to play three separate one-week engagements—in Montclair, New Jersey; the Bronx; and Brooklyn. I was given a fine coach, and I studied with him, in the empty hall, every day, all day. He would say, "Now, here's a chair, and you walk around it on entrance." Or "Your male nurse enters from stage left. You turn and say—" I was quietly realizing what I'd gotten into. But I plodded on. And I did learn the lines. But I had never met the cast or seen the set since the Frank Fay opening years before, and was completely naive about stage deportment, acting, makeup, wardrobe, cues, timing—in fact, the only thing I was sure of was the exit from the theater!

On opening night, in Montclair, the people who'd watched me die at the Greenwich Village Inn all bought tickets, and this time they brought their friends, and children. The locals were there, and Broadway had come en masse from Lindy's, the Stage Deli, Toots Shor's, and every other watering hole within 100 miles of this expected disaster.

I stood in the wings, awaiting my cue, wearing a suit, vintage, early thirties; pancake on my face; and gray gook in my hair (which wouldn't need it today). Ten seconds before my entrance, I would have given my life's earnings not to walk on! I thought there would have to be a slight delay—such as my lifetime. But on I went! I felt stiff and wooden as I worked with a cast I had not met until just before curtain. But I remembered the lines, and I made the right stage moves! (Hey, Charlie! Strike a medal!) When it was over, finally, the people in the audience applauded, but were, according to witnesses, dumbstruck. "The son-of-a-bitch got through it!" I still treasure the Variety review of that opening. It says, "Barry Gray Disappoints Broadway Mob—Clicks in Harvey"!

I retired from the theater after the three-week run. I have received other offers, but at this writing, never again! My respect for the working actor climbed to the stratosphere. God! What a tough buck! How much you have to know! My comments on the air have been considerably tempered since then. I recommend an acting experience to every would-be critic before he writes his first line. It cuts you down to size. The only humor I can find is in seeing Harvey on the screen many years later, played by Jimmy Stewart. As I left the theater, I uttered the cliché of every actor who didn't get the part. Asked what I thought of Stewart's performance, I replied, "He didn't understand the role!"

The Chandler's euphoria lasted until l'affaire Josephine Baker and then the Winchell attacks, and as has been noted, business plunged sharply, television went, and the studio intermittently became my broadcast home—but only after a few brief, tentative tries in other saloons. The saloons didn't "play," for the audience wanted to see and hear stars, and stars were not dropping in. The goon squad had done its work well, and innocently enough, some just didn't "want to get involved." And in looking back over the years, calmly, in some cases I ask, "Why should they have gotten involved?"

I worked in the studio for some months—it may have been a year; I truly don't recall, and the time is of minor importance—but I do remember the period of Coventry well. Lindy's was just downstairs, and I didn't go there— or anywhere else. I walked to the parking lot directly across the street, reached my car, lifted the hood to check the engine for tampering, closed the hood, got into the car, and drove home—each night, as much as possible, by a different route. The police had drummed the lessons of prevention into me well. When you're sitting in a theater and someone takes the seat behind you—move. When walking or driving, look for a tail. Don't form habits of dining at the same place, at the same time. Arrive at the studio at different times—and so forth, and so forth. The only time I was a pigeon was on leaving the studio, but that was right on Broadway, and there were a lot of people. I thought it safe. It wasn't.

For after a couple of months I received the offer to

originate the program from Hutton's restaurant. WMCA liked the idea and I opened, and for the first time worked on percentage. My income, as I've noted, would depend on whatever business arrived from 11 P.M. until closing time. Those were exciting nights. It was during the period when the margarine heir Mickey Jelke was accused of being a pimp, and his lady of the evening was singing, loudly, for the vice cops. A lot of famous names were her reputed clients. John Carradine was named. He denied it from my dais, and called the lady a "whore." There was little doubt of that. But it was the first time the word had been used on the air. We were getting an "X" rating in radio!

I was also, as I've noted, getting a short count from the boss. Each night the room was filled with diners and drinkers, and each week I would be told, "They weren't spenders." Or "The money isn't around." From where I sat, five feet above the audience, on a tiny dais, they looked as though they were "knocking 'em back" pretty rapidly—but who can argue with a cashier whose eyes are too close together?

I took two weeks off, and columnist-commentator Victor Riesel sat in for me. I went to Palm Springs. About a week later, at 4 A.M. California time, the ringing phone jolted me out of sleep, and I was told that Riesel had been tailed from Hutton's to Lindy's. Finished with his meal, he left and walked out. Around the corner of 51st Street, he was called by name. He turned. His attacker threw some liquid in his face, and then fled. Riesel was brought back into Lindy's and laid on the floor. They called an ambulance, and everyone said, "Don't touch him. The doctors will know what to do." If there had been one former Boy Scout in the group, tragedy could have been averted, because milk, or even plain water, dropped in Riesel's eyes would have saved his sight. As he lay there, the acid did its work. Riesel, by the time he was treated professionally, was blind!

I flew back to New York, while politicos from Governor Harriman down visited Riesel in the hospital. There were many "why's" to be answered, and to this day there are questions. But it was stated that Riesel had incurred the wrath of underworld labor bosses because of his columns and comments on their nefarious deals. He had been warned, and he had ignored the warnings. He was an easy target for them when they found he was to be sitting in for me, at the same place and same time, each night. Later, there was talk of "a man at the bar who came in each night and watched him—and left when he did." If that's true, it can be assumed that Riesel was tailed, and his habits observed.

The "man at the bar" was never found. There were reports that his attackers had been slain by his employers in the "hit." But New York is a one-day-sensation society, and the story faded. I'm sure that Riesel and I agree on one thing. The story was never resolved successfully, nor were the real culprits caught. It was, and it remains, tragedy, which may be alleviated somewhat by the very recent news that Riesel may regain partial sight through surgery. That would indeed be blessed news to hear!

I went back to Hutton's and climbed the broadcast dais again. Came another anniversary on WMCA during that period, and Hutton's decided to have a party. The restaurant would bake a nine-tier cake. We would have Earl Wilson and Florence Henderson to officiate. And at the stroke of midnight, the audience would sing "Happy Anniversary" while Hutton's maître d', named Peter, would climb the dais and with candles blazing from the tiered cake, smile for the photographer, who would then rush the negative to the *New York Post* for publication the next day.

The witching hour came. The audience sang. Peter ascended the steps leading up to the guests and microphones. The photographer, having our group and Peter, with cake, in his sights, yelled, "Hold it!" Peter, holding the enormous cake, turned his best profile to the camera.

A lady in the audience yelled, "Oh, my God!" The cake was sliding down its tray, like a ship being launched. It left the chef's base, did a double flip in the air, dropped eight feet, and hit a man directly below it on the back of his neck. The man, who turned out to be a doctor, was wearing a navy blue suit.

Peter rushed down the steps and, grabbing a dry napkin, started to wipe the whipped cream and cake from the man's neck, shirt, and back. The dry napkin merely smeared the mess into the fabric of his suit, while the doctor kept beating at Peter's hands, yelling, "Get away from me, you dumb bastard!" The tape of that broadcast relives the moment from the woman's cry to a peal of laughter from Florence Henderson that lasted for two minutes. She later said, "It was the funniest thing I have ever seen!"

The doctor sued Hutton's. I hear the case was settled. By then I was gone from the scene, permanently. For a New Year's Eve had come and gone. That night the restaurant had been packed to the doors. The check given me the next payday did not reflect the New Year's mob. Again I was told, "It didn't add up to what we thought it would." 'Bye!

After that, and regularly, I have been asked to originate the program from this place or that. Save one other time, years later, the answer has been no. The program lost something outside the studio walls. Granted that the noise and "now" presence of a live and lively audience has its pluses, and that strange and dramatic things sometimes happen, a much better program is obtained, on balance, within the studio walls. Your guests are of a higher caliber, and they address the microphones, rather than the crowd. And radio, in the words of that early Los Angeles mentor, is "for one pair of ears alone."

That one exception referred to was my return to Miami Beach, to the Seville Hotel. It was brand-new then. And it provided two enormous suites on the top floor, terraces facing the Atlantic, all food, gratuities, excellent fee, and the use of the late Gabriel Heatter's telephone line to New York, where my program was broadcast locally on WMCA and also put on the Mutual network for stations across the country to carry. It got us interesting mail from Olympia, Washington, and Winslow, Arizona!

Nearby, in Coral Gables, actors Rip Torn and Maureen Stapleton were opening in a new play. They were invited to be guests, and to arrive at 11 P.M., when we went on the air. They were coming right from dress rehearsal, and would be hungry. I promised they would be interviewed and then fed. I told the captain what they looked like, to be watching out for them, and to let me know the instant they arrived so they could be put on the air promptly, and no waiting.

The hour of 11 arrived. No guests. I talked to myself and to the full network for twenty minutes, and then discovered Torn and Stapleton at the bar, happening to spot them through the dim gloom of the room. The captain, it seems, had no doubt turned his back, to palm a

$5 tip, and they had just walked past him and gone to the bar. There they had had three quick ones to ease the pain of rehearsal.

I introduced them, and immediately knew I was in great danger. Rip Torn, tired from his grueling day of rehearsal, no food, and liquor on an empty stomach, looked mean, and Maureen, tired from her grueling day of rehearsal, no food, and liquor on an empty stomach, looked bombed. Her eyes were dull, and she looked as though she could have been anywhere and was. I decided, nervously, to concentrate on Rip. We had never met before. In my nervousness, I asked him the dumbest question imaginable, and one he had been asked at least a thousand times: "What's your real name?" He glared at me, and snarled, "What's yours?" I thought he was going to belt me. We had a ball for about five minutes and the interview was over. Maureen throughout just smiled, a cross between ZaSu Pitts and Mona Lisa.

Oddly, among all the thousands of guests who've sat at the mikes, few have been "under the influence." Robert Mitchum, an old friend, and Vincent Price, another friend of vintage standing, came to the studio one night, both with their public relations people and arriving from different restaurants. They had been given the "grind tour" by their respective picture companies that day. They'd been started on the *Today* show; they had been run through every talk show in New York, not to mention countless newspaper and magazine interviews; and finally, I had them, after dinner and after many, many drinks to lift their spirits and calm their fatigue.

They sat down, both in fine form, and we had talked for about two minutes when someone mentioned the late Humphrey Bogart. They immediately started to tell "Bogey" stories, which were great—except that the stories made them cry, on each other, with the arms of each holding the other straight. It went on for a long time—at least, it seemed so. It was absolutely the first crying jag broadcast complete on radio. They left, and each called the next day to apologize. There was no need. They are both remarkable men. Price is urbane, witty, informed. Mitchum is all of that, plus macho personified.

I remember his arrival in New York one night when that rag *Confidential* had done a job on him. He came to see me, and when I got off the air he said, "You know where that bastard publisher is? Tell me—I want to pull his fuckin' arm out of its socket!" He meant it.

But let's go back to the grind that major studios and publishers put their stars through when they bring them through Manhattan "on tour." Mitchum and Price taught me a lesson. Not since that night have I accepted a guest who has been "bicycled" around town and arrives dead beat at my door late at night. It is not fair to him. Nor is it fair to me, for he has been wrung out. And the listeners are being hustled. By now they have a feeling they've heard that voice all day, everywhere, and it is counterproductive, it seems to me, for it becomes, for the listener or prospective reader, an irritant, a turn-off, and hurts the sale of tickets and books. Another thing that boils me is the interviewer who says, "I haven't read your book—tell me about it." Or he uses the euphemistic term, "I have 'skimmed' your book—can you fill me in?" How the hell can you talk to an author about his book which you haven't read?

Jack Warden, a fine actor, was involved in a case in point. He was appearing in Robert Shaw's *Man in the Glass Booth*. Shaw had written it first as a book about Eichmann, the now executed master planner of Hitler's "Final Solution"—the mass extermination of the Jews.

The play takes place on a set reproducing the Israeli courtroom where Eichmann, for security reasons, testified in a booth of bulletproof glass, for obviously some of the people in the courtroom would have loved to kill him right there. Israel wanted legal justice done. At any rate, Warden went on to be interviewed by a radio dunce who'd neither read the book nor seen the play. And his introduction was "Jack Worlen." He then asked, "Tell me, what's it like to be sitting up there in the glass booth, calling those plays?" He thought Warden played a sportscaster!

The guest who truly had me nervous was the late Lenny Bruce. I had known Lenny for years, as a young, extraordinarily good-looking man who hung around the corner of 51st and Seventh in New York, which was the site of Hanson's drugstore, the so-called "poor performer's Lindy's." It was always filled with comics, showgirls (who bought their makeup there, and stopped for coffee and trade talk), and the hangers-on. Lenny's career started to move, and he came to full flower at the Blue Angel. I finally went to see him, never having previously watched him work. I wanted to find out what the fuss was about. He works blue? Dirty? How blue? How dirty? I went. On the way I met one of Broadway's best-known hookers, with her John. When Lenny had been introduced and was two minutes into his act, she got up and swept out, followed by her friend, and as she went past me she was muttering, "Dirtiest thing I've ever heard!"

After his performance, which was brilliant, albeit earthy, I went backstage. In a moment, another comic, "Fat Jack" E. Leonard, came into the dressing room. Fat Jack had been the first to meet me on the street, mumble something, and run when the Winchell blasts began. For years he had been a regular attender at the broadcasts.

Since Winchell, we'd not seen each other. We did not say hello.

Lenny was complimented on his bravura performance, and he said to me, "Man, I dig your show. Right here I listen every night when I'm not on. When can I come on?" I hesitated. He picked it up at once and said, "I'll work clean—honest; you'll love it!" It was Saturday night. My show was then on from midnight until 2, and Lenny was booked for Tuesday at 1.

At 12:50 he walked into the studio. On the air, in the first hour, I was talking with the educational and political mentor of the Puerto Rican community, Joseph Monserrat, and a black Black African from Sierra Leone who had been Oxford-educated and was at the U.N. They were having a high-level, small-mouth, carefully enunciated discussion of the employment opportunities, or lack of them, for the brown and black people of America. Lenny sat in the corner, but with his legs crossed, the suspended leg going like a metronome. Finally he could stand it no longer. He jumped up and pushed himself between the two men, and said, "I've been listening to you two cats talk for ten minutes. Whatya gonna do for the Spics and Spades?" Then the news came on. I worked the next hour alone.

My engineer loved the Lenny Bruce intrusion into the interview. He was a black man. But a few nights later he was to lose a lot of pigment temporarily in a hurry. On Madison Avenue one summer afternoon, I met a Hollywood moviemaker who dealt in nickel-and-dime productions. His newest dealt with Boy Meets Girl, Girl Goes to Africa. She is attacked by a Lion. Boy saves Girl. Girl gives herself to Boy rather than the Lion. He asked if I would do him a favor—oh, not to put the "stars" on the air, but how about an "interview" with the lion? "What d'ya mean?" "Oh, just have the lion come into the studio, and let him stalk around for a minute, and then we can take him outside the next afternoon and grab a couple of pictures of you holding the mike up to the lion, as though he were being interviewed." He was an old friend, and I'm a sucker for a bad picture. I okayed the lion's appearance for the next night.

My producer had booked three Jewish gentlemen from the Anti-Defamation League to talk of Middle Eastern conditions. They arrived shortly before air time and sat comfortably along the left wall of the studio, awaiting the beginning of the program. My black engineer sat behind the control-room glass fiddling with his gadgets and awaiting his cue. At that moment the studio door swung open, and a large lion's mane started through the door. My three Jewish guests saw only the lion's head, and I thought they would fight to go up the air vent directly above their heads. Around the lion's neck was a large steel collar, and from it extended two thick chains, which were held firmly by the lion's two handlers. They were strong men, with thick forearms and enormous biceps. The lion, as he strained at his leashes, pulled them around the room as though they were toys. He was about eight feet long and had enormous paws and a huge head, with big, luminous, jungle-lit eyes. He cased the studio quickly, saw me, and padded around until he got to within licking and smelling distance of my right elbow. My guests were almost in the air vent, and near hysterics, for they thought, After he eats Barry, we're next!

The lion sniffed me, licked my elbow, didn't care for it, and backed off to turn his head to the right, and *then* he spied the engineer. Now he was not only a black man, but a blue-black man. The lion stalked to the control-room glass and stood on his hind legs, and his forepaws now reached the studio ceiling as he peered through the glass at the engineer—who put it this way later: "He looked at me as though to say, 'I knew your folks back home'!" We went on the air, I mentioned the lion's presence, I talked with the movie man for a couple of minutes, and they left. My ADL guests spoke in tremulous voices throughout their time on the air, and my engineer still looked Revlon gray. That lion certainly was impressive. I wonder why the heroine of the film ever threw him over for the boy!

Time passed, and I invited Ann Corio onto the broadcast. As a girl she had been one of America's most celebrated and most beautiful strippers. As a woman, she was beautiful, and planning a road show, *This Was Burlesque*, which was to become a national hit. She arrived at the broadcast accompanied by a male singer. I wondered where her husband was.

I got the story later. The three of them had dined together. There was a spat. She rose from the table and said, "I'm going to Barry Gray's—are you coming?" The husband replied with the equivalent of "Drop dead!" She turned to the singer and said, "Would you escort me?" He replied, "Of course," and rose from the table, and they left together, leaving one enraged husband.

Ann was now on the air with me. My studio is large, and contains six small tables, each with a microphone. The tables are set in a large circle, and when I have one guest, he or she sits directly opposite me, a distance of about eight feet. That way I can address or listen to the guest and at the same time can see the engineer and the producer, over the guest's shoulder, through the control-room glass. Along the left wall there are comfortable chairs, about eight, in which visitors may lounge. To my left also, but at the front of the studio—in short, as far as you can get from my microphone—is the sound-lock door which allows one to enter and exit.

On the night I spoke with Ann Corio, there were also chairs on my right. In one of these, the male singer reclined. I asked Ann, "What was it like to take your clothes off while more than two thousand pairs of eyes looked at you—or perhaps leered?" (This was long before *Oh! Calcutta!*) Before she could reply, the studio door swung open. There stood her husband, tanked, and he looked across the room at the male singer. There he was —that bastard who had walked off with his wife! And he plunged across the studio, grabbed the singer's shirt, and belted him. They then started to roll on the floor, in a full-fledged battle to the death.

My interview with Ann Corio continued without a reference to the grunts and groans emanating from the floor while the two combatants did battle, all audible to the air audience, who probably thought they were getting my program along with a New Jersey station broadcasting fights, or wrestling. The interview and the combat ended almost at the same time, and they all left together. Ultimately the marriage was dissolved. And I strongly suspect that that is the only edge on fight broadcasting I can claim over Howard Cosell!

Just about the biggest faux pas I have ever made took place in the La Scala restaurant in Manhattan. Red Buttons had become a father for the first time about three months earlier. His wife was in Los Angeles. I took him to dinner with publicist Judy Tarlo from London, who had been my producer, and my then grown, but not yet married, daughter. Across the room sat a young couple— the man, with his back to us, wearing shoulder-length hair —with an older, distinguished-looking gentleman. Red excused himself to go to the washroom. My daughter rose and said, "I'll go to the ladies' room." Returning, Red stopped at the table across the way and started an animated conversation. He then reached into his inside pocket and started to show the trio at the table pictures of his baby. He returned to our table and said, "That's Sidney Lumet and his wife [Lena Horne's daughter], and Walter Wanger."

Parenthetically, Wanger had accosted a Hollywood mogul named Jennings Lang in a Beverly Hills parking lot during daylight shopping hours and, suspecting Lang of fragrant deliciousness with Wanger's wife, Wanger shot Lang in the groin.

Back at La Scala: I said to Red, "That's Sidney Lumet? Where the hell did he get all that hair?" I had met Lumet in London, during his direction of *The Hill*, where I'd gone to interview its stars, Sean Connery and Ossie Davis, and with that I rose and walked to their table. We greeted each other, and Sidney introduced me to Walter Wanger. Red had come back to the table. I pointed to him, and said, "Is he boring you with his baby pictures? Let me show you what *I've* done for my country"—and turning, I waved my daughter to the table. "Sidney, Mrs. Lumet, may I present my daughter, Melodie, and this"—pointing to Wanger—"is Jennings Lang"!

I was standing across the table from Red, and as I said that I saw him blanch, and his eyes crossed. We went back to our table, and I asked, "What's wrong?" He said, "Do ya know what you said?" I shook my head. He said, "You introduced Walter Wanger as Jennings Lang!" I felt myself go white, and every pore in my body opened. I gasped, "Oh, no!" I quickly jumped up to apologize. They were going out the door of the restaurant. Red said, "Forget it, you shmuck, you'll only make it worse." The next time I saw Wanger, he was on the Isle of Capri, walking arm in arm with Hedy Lamarr. He saw me, and looked right through me. I wonder why.

The first time I went to London, I had the company of Jack Carter and his wife. The four of us had made a deal with KLM Royal Dutch Airlines to fly there, in exchange for advertising. It is called in our business "a trade-out." Very common, and used by every quiz show and interview show in America that brings guests in from faraway places. I simply had to go on WMCA and say that I was going to London as "a guest of KLM Royal Dutch Airlines." That was it.

Jack was doing a comedy series on Channel 5 in New York. He and his director enjoyed a mutual hatred. Jack tried to work a few airline jokes into a comedy routine, and every time "KLM" was mentioned, the director struck it with a blue pencil. The countdown was getting tight. Departure was about a week away, and the airline had not gotten its plug from Jack. There was but one television show to go before Jack was to take off for London, if he could deliver that plug. (Although I'm quite sure they would've taken him anyway.) The last show had an airliner fuselage on the set, without company markings of any kind. It had to do with a routine of departing passengers for somewhere—kind of a comedy version of *Airport*. Jack tried again, and again, to get "KLM" into the jokes. No way. They had their dress rehearsal. It was three hours to air time. The set went dark, and everyone went to dinner. Jack sneaked onto the set, and with thick chalk wrote "KLM" heavily in white on everything he could find. When they turned up the lights for the show, Jack had delivered his plug fifty times over.

The comedy show was canceled, but we did go to London. We flew first to Amsterdam, and had "technical trouble" there, and Jack picked up a bottle of the local gin called "Focking" and said, "This is what we've been getting!" By arrival time in London, we were wiped out, but that night Danny Kaye was opening at the Palladium, and we had tickets, obtained under enormous pull, for the performance. We duly bathed, shaved, and dressed. Our ladies got beautiful, and off we went. Nothing but tea sandwiches before the theater, and suffering air lag and exhaustion. The Palladium was bedlam when Danny Kaye was introduced. The audience was a dressed movie set—black tie, exquisite evening gowns on the ladies—and sitting next to me was a lady whose attire put them all away. She was topped by an enormous, glittering diamond tiara!

I could see that Danny was brilliant for fifteen minutes. Oh, I'm sure he was brilliant for his total time onstage—but the lights of the stage, the warmth of the theater, and my total fatigue couldn't withstand the pull of sleep. I curled up on Lady Tiara's shoulder. She kept shrugging me away. I would find a new hollow, or niche, and slumber some more.

The show was now over, with cheering, huzzahs, and flowers, and as the audience filed out, Danny's aide came to our aisle and said, "Danny would like you to come backstage." We followed him, and were asked to wait for a moment outside, as he was expecting a brief visit from royalty. An instant later, my seatmate, my sleeping bag, Lady Tiara swept imperiously by, and as the door opened and Danny greeted his guest with "Your Majesty —I am honored," I found that I had been sleeping on the Queen Mother of Bulgaria—or Rumania—or Transylvania—but she was a queen. And I had slept on her. Thank God! Not *with* her. Her shoulders were bony as hell!

Otto Preminger, the film director, had been on the air with me often over the years, and we had gotten along well. In fact, it was Otto who, on hearing of my father's death, rushed into the WMCA breach and sat in my chair and conducted the program while I went to Los Angeles. One day the phone rang and it was Otto's press agent, Nat Rudick. Rudick asked if Otto could come on the air and talk about his new film, *Advise and Consent*, which had just opened. I explained to Nat that I liked Otto, but I had not cared for the film. Nat thanked me for my candor, and we said goodbye. A few moments later, another call came in from Rudick, who said, "I've just talked with Otto, and he said, 'What're friends for?' He'd like to come on the air, and you'll tell him what you didn't like about the film, and you'll discuss it." I said, "Fine, as long as he understands the rules of the game, for I generally don't have people on the air whose picture or book I don't like. What purpose is served to have the guest come on and then rap his project?" Rudick said, "I agree—but Otto really wants the opportunity to exchange points of view with you." The date was set.

Preminger appeared: we went on the air, just the two of us; and I introduced Otto in glowing terms, saving the worst for last. I pointed out that he had broken the censorship barrier with his then bold dialogue in *The Moon Is Blue* and plot of *The Man with the Golden Arm*, and listed all of his many, many deserved credits for films he had directed. I ended my introduction with, "and his newest film is *Advise and Consent*—which, unfortunately, I didn't care for."

From across the broadcast desk: "Vat do you know, you idiot?" Preminger continued in his blast of me for half an hour, barely pausing for a hyphen. I sat and listened, with a feeble attempt to remonstrate from time to time. I was being ground under by the Austrian-born tank. He attacked my point of view, my ignorance of film, my presence on the air, my taxable income (he said he paid more than I do—he does), and intimated strongly that my mother and father had never married, and if they had, their issue had been dropped on its head often. Such was our "exchange of views."

After a pause for news, during which he glared at me, I finally suggested we take telephone calls from the listeners to get their opinions on the film and on the Preminger point of view. He readily agreed. Both sides of the phoned-in conversation could be heard on the air. First call: "I'm one who lives in Forest Hills," said the lady, "and I will never go to see a Preminger film again! He's a rude boor!" Second call: "Preminger stinks! And he has no manners!" Third call: "Well, rat. Preminger really nailed ya—he's great!" And so they went through the program. When I was attacked, Preminger beamed. When he was vilified, he sometimes took the phone and attempted a dialogue with the caller. Most callers hadn't seen the film, and vowed they wouldn't. Some were delighted to hold coats while we fought—they loved hearing a fight between two people, on anything. The program ended. I left, half an hour later, with Preminger still on the phone hearing complaints and kudos.

The next day the mail started to arrive, and it kept coming for three more days. On that last day I received, by hand, a small packet of envelopes, eight in all, addressed to "Otto Preminger, Columbia Pictures, 711 Fifth Avenue, New York, N.Y." I read them. They were all attacks on me, congratulating Otto for "pinning that creep's ears back," or saying, "Someone finally told him off, and I love you for it." There was even one suggestion that the Constitution be changed so that foreign-born Otto could run for President.

I laughed at "Otto's Revenge." That night on the air I told of the hand-delivered packet of letters, and what they said. And then added that I had some three hundred letters in my office which said exactly the opposite. The writers hated Preminger and detested his uncouth conduct on the air. My telephone rang the next day. I recognized Otto's voice at once as he said, "Barry? You have three hundred letters in your office attacking me?" I said, "Yes, Otto." He asked, "May I send a messenger for them?" I said, "Of course—do you want to read them?" And he snapped back, "No! Count them!" And hung up!

Weeks later, when the air had cleared, I invited Otto back onto the program, to match opinions with Victor Riesel, now in recovered health, but blind. They sat around my circular broadcast desk, but approximately facing each other. Riesel, with the auditory acuteness developed by the sightless, addressed Preminger across the table. At each man's elbow there was a carafe containing water, and beside it, a paper cup filled with water. The discussion grew heated on some minute point the immaculately dressed Preminger made to Riesel about Germany. One statement led quickly to another, and their voices rose. Finally Riesel demanded, "Are you calling me a Nazi?" And with that he picked up his cup of water and flung its contents full in Otto's face. Riesel couldn't see, but he could sure pitch! He hit Preminger head on, got up, and accompanied by his wife, started to stomp out of the studio. Their raised voices, now off mike, were heard clearly by the audience. From the door the argument raged. Finally, as things got cleared up, they subsided. They went back to their seats, and the program continued as Otto, from time to time, mopped his drenched lapels, shirt, and tie with his handkerchief. With it all, I have found Otto to be an urbane, sophisticated, informed man, with a great deal of personal charm. But pray God, I'll never have to work for him!

Back in my Miami days, when most of America thought that President Harry Truman was a sure loser, I had supported his candidacy, cheered his courage, applauded his foreign policy, and followed his campaign with enormous interest and plenty of air comments. I put my money up, too. And when Mr. Truman beat Dewey, I was wildly elated. Not so most Floridians.

Back in New York, and a few days before the President was about to make way for Dwight Eisenhower, I mentioned to an attorney, the noted civil libertarian Morris Ernst, that I had tremendous admiration for Truman, and told him some of the anecdotes of the past. Some Dade County (Miami area) officials had been so incensed at his victory, and infuriated by my support, that the night following the election a "strange" water seepage was discovered under the Copa, the club from which I was broadcasting. A digging crew dug a ditch 6 feet deep and 4 feet wide around the club, so the only way one could enter was to walk across planks. Beautifully dressed people did that exact thing every night. After a week of "looking," the seepage was discovered somewhere else, and the ditch was filled in. When the Kefauver Committee came to Florida, with subpoena power, it asked one of those public officials how he happened to have $72,000 in a tin box in his closet. "Where did it come from?" The modestly paid official thought for a moment, and said, "My wife's a careful shopper"!

Ernst asked me if I would like to meet the outgoing President. "And how!" So a couple of days later, he took me to the White House. We entered through a side door and went into President Truman's office. The walls were bare, with all the pictures having been taken down to be shipped to Independence. Practically all that remained in that seat of power and prestige was the presidential desk and some chairs. When we entered, I was introduced to the President. The dapper Chief Executive jumped up, came around the desk, and shook my very nervous hand. He asked, "Aren't you the young man that's hated by Walter Winchell and Drew Pearson?" I said, "Yes." He gave me the supreme accolade—"You must be a remarkable person!" He then asked us to be seated. I asked how he felt about leaving the White House. He replied, "Great!" And added, "I rubbed some of the shine off the stars of that poor bastard Eisenhower!" He paused and said, "He hasn't the vaguest idea of what this job's about."

I thought of it years later, when a comic named Jackie Kannon, who died too young at 48, did his act in the then famed Ratfink Room in New York. Jackie would say, "I liked Eisenhower when he was President. He didn't fool around with politics—he just hooked and sliced!"

Practically every Representative in the House has dropped by my microphones at one time or another, and countless Senators. But Bob Kennedy was the one who made news. He entered the New York senatorial race with cries of "carpetbagger," "invader"—and those were *just* the things you could print, or say. He opposed Senator Kenneth Keating, a kindly man, first our ambassador to India and now our ambassador to Israel (in politics, when you lose, you win).

Keating, sanguine at Kennedy's first announcement and privately confident of beating him, started to witness a switch, a dramatic one, about three weeks before election day. Bob was making tremendous inroads in "safe" Keating country. The polls were giving Keating bad news, and it was getting worse by the hour. Advisers told Keating to take to television heavily. He bought time all over the tube.

Kennedy stuck to radio, and a lot of that radio was with me—and free, of course. We became friendly. I liked the fact that he never dodged a question, or skirted it. He answered you dead on, and looked you in the eye. He was one hell of a guy. Keating, meanwhile, was getting hysterical on television. Four nights before election day he bought an hour on a network station and thundered, "I've invited my opposition to debate with me, and instead of his presence, I have but this empty chair!" At which he would point dramatically to the chair next to him. He continued—"I will be on CBS tomorrow night for one hour, and I defy him to face me then before these cameras, and you!"

There was great activity at Kennedy's private planning preserve in the Hotel Carlyle. I had ridden the Kennedy campaign car that day, with a tape machine, and watched the outpouring of people just wanting to see the candidate, to touch him, to cheer him. One black lady in Harlem clung to his hand as Kennedy stood on the trunk of the car, while aides held his feet to prevent his being pulled into the street. The black lady finally dug her fingers into the back of his hand with her fingernails, and actually ripped away shallow troughs of skin. She yelled, "I've got a souvenir! I've got a souvenir!" Kennedy bled intermittently for quite a while.

That night the heavy Democratic power was there in his hotel suite, headed by his confidante and the ablest man in state politics, former Governor–Ambassador–Presidential Adviser Averell Harriman. The plans were formulated, and we skulked out of the hotel through a side entrance to avoid the press. We drove in small groups, in many cars, to the CBS Television Center on West 57th Street, near the West Side Highway of New York. We arrived a bit too early, so Kennedy strolled down the street with his familiar walk, hands in pockets, deep in thought. His aide, William vanden Heuvel, walked with me. Coming toward Kennedy was a young man. He passed Kennedy, after first glancing at his face. Then he stopped, turned around to stare, and perceptibly shrugged his shoulders, as though to say to himself, "It couldn't be he—what he hell would *he* be doing here, alone, on a deserted street at this hour?"

Three minutes later, we entered the CBS studios. One press representative yelled, "Are you gonna debate Keating?" Kennedy replied, with a wry smile, "I don't know—he's been doing pretty well with that chair!" In fact, he was there to pick up the gauntlet, and he attempted to walk onto the television set as Keating made his opening comments.

Kennedy and his group were stopped at the door by CBS officials, who said that Keating had paid for the hour and Kennedy was not listed as a participant on the program. So Keating's ploy was proved fraudulent. He *wanted* to debate that chair. But Kennedy knew the game. He had purchased the half hour immediately following Keating's hour! Many members of the press, who had seen him being barred from Keating's program, fol-lowed Kennedy to watch his studio being set up. They also covered the TV monitors, directly outside, to see and hear what Keating was saying. By now, it was obvious Keating had been informed by an aide what was going on outside. He looked flustered, rattled, and off his form.

Down the hall, the cameras were being set up for the Kennedy appearance. Leland Hayward, the Broadway producer, was in charge. The cameraman focused the shot and then stepped aside for Hayward to okay it. Hayward said, "Give me a little more Kennedy." The cameraman said, "But that'll take Gray out of the shot." (Kennedy had asked for me to conduct the interview.) Hayward sweetly said, "*He's* not running for office, is he?"

Kennedy's half hour went brilliantly. As he was coming out of the studios with his wife, Ethel, pictures were taken by the dozen, and a mob of well-wishers formed. It was a triumph that was sweetened by the news that Keating had run from his studio and an aide had turned over a large flowerpot to keep the press from pursuing him. The newspapers, the next day, reported the entire event, with pictures of Keating's back as he ran away, and in the foreground the huge roadblock flowerpot.

The next evening, at 7, my phone rang. Kennedy would like to debate Keating, on my program, that night! In four hours we had acceptances from both sides, the press had been alerted, and by air time the studio, halls, and offices of WMCA were packed with the greatest number of reporters, photographers, and radio and tele-vision people I have ever seen at one time in one place. When we went on the air the crush was so tight that around my feet, and those of the candidates, reporters and aides were sitting on the floor.

Both candidates were nervously careful, with the result

that they were not too exciting. The only humor came when Kennedy asked Keating, "What will you do about Sabah?" (Everyone looked at someone else—Sabah? What the hell is a Sabah?) Kennedy's question dealt with a jutting piece of geography that arrowheads into the South China Sea and lies next to the Philippines. There was then political turmoil there—sparsely covered by some papers, not at all in others. Obviously Keating hadn't done his minute homework. He stumbled, shuffled papers, and finally weaseled into another question.

When the debate was over, after two hours, it had covered the major issues, brought sharp but brief exchanges between the two candidates, and provided listeners the opportunity to hear their differences on key issues in the election. The next day, every New York newspaper carried a report of the debate, with pictures. Page 1, column 1. It broke on wire services, was seen on television news programs, and was carried by every radio station everywhere. Keating and Kennedy had finally met.

It had been a stroke of campaign genius on Kennedy's part to time the debate as he did—and on radio. For when the returns were in, I asked one Kennedy aide, "Why radio?" And he looked at me, his eyes twinkled, and he replied, "How well do you think it would've gone on television? This white-haired, distinguished Senator from New York, an incumbent, versus a heavy-haired, tousled youngster from out of state—Keating might've won on sympathy alone. On radio they were on equal ground!"

The hours were narrowing down to election day, and as I recall there were but two more broadcasts of mine scheduled before the polls opened. The first of these was an interview with a pro-Keating man. I cannot remember his name, but he came out blasting Kennedy, using as the basis for his attack the fact that Bob had served as junior counsel to the Joseph McCarthy committee early in his political career. He didn't spell it out but he implied that Kennedy was now, and had always been, pro-McCarthy.

I despised McCarthy, his tone, his innuendo, his smears, and his inability to back any of it with fact. He was a disgrace to the body politic, and I said so at every opportunity. I didn't care for the idea of Kennedy's minimal counsel role in those early days—but I had gotten to know and understand the tremendous growth of the man. He was tough, and honest, and had moved from political naiveté to great understanding of the problems of the poor, the ill-housed, the blacks, the browns, the used itinerant workers of the land. They recognized the truth and dignity of him, and felt as one with him. And now I had this lip-licking guest across from me denying the Kennedy climb from the valley of rich ignorance to the peak of understanding of what ills this country was undergoing. I asked him again and again to spell out his charges of present pro-McCarthyism against Kennedy. He weaseled. And finally, after he had twisted and dodged to the point of my utter frustration, I said, "You're an oily man." And bade him good night.

Early the next morning, the general manager of WMCA (at that time) awakened me by his telephone call, and summoned me to the WMCA lawyers' offices at once. I think I was there by 10 A.M. I was summarily suspended from my broadcast because of the use of the word "oily." To this day I shake my head about that.

So while every front page in town, and most in the country, were filled with news of the famed debate on WMCA, I was off the air. The final night, Ed Brown, a newsman, sat in my chair. The night before election!

And the following day, the people of the State of New York registered a firm and resounding "Yes!" to Kennedy. That night, shortly after the polls closed, when the returns were first trickling in and long before Bob knew whether he had been successful or not, I went to his campaign headquarters. As I walked in, he was surrounded by hopeful well-wishers. He saw me at once, and summoned me to a corner of the room, where we could speak privately. His first words to me were "I hear I got you in trouble!" Here was a man with his political future in the balance who was worried about *my* trouble, and what he thought *he* had done! I have a photograph of that moment, which someone snapped and later sent me. It shows Kennedy listening in rapt attention, and my hand is moving in a gesture as I explained what *I* had said. At the moment when, at the far end of the room, a television set was projecting the election returns, Kennedy was listening to my story of travail. As I say—this was a man!

Thousands of letters poured into WMCA. I was suspended for six nights. My fine? I had to pay the postage for all the letters of regret the station sent to listeners explaining my radio absence. I wrestled with the decision whether to go back on the air, but I have learned all through the ensuing years that it was the right thing to do. For never since has there been a repeat of that performance by any member of management, and never, save for that one time, has there been a rebuke by the station for a program, a guest, a comment. Nor has there ever been a directive about whom to have on the air, what to say, or what not to say. It is, and has been for a very long time, a one-to-one relationship. If I have a problem or a question, or want to take some time off, I talk to the boss, Peter Straus. I get a fast yes or no. Compare that with the memos, politics, and intrigue that go on throughout the broadcast business at every level, and the higher you rise, the worse it gets.

So now it was Senator Robert Kennedy. I was back on the air. And we saw each other from time to time, but always on the air—save once, when I was invited to dinner and asked my opinion about an upcoming election. I wasn't flattered; I was sure that the Senator was asking everyone he met essentially the same questions. What did amuse me was his coming to the program a few nights later to speak for the candidate of his party, New York's present mayor, Abe Beame. He spoke for twenty minutes, and pulled out all the stops. When he finished, I asked him, "Senator—I have listened to your enthusiastic comment, and fervor, about Abe Beame for twenty minutes. Do you believe you can remove your mantle and lay it across Abe's shoulders and get him votes?"

He looked at me for a long moment, and answered. "No." He was right. Beame lost that earlier election.

Weeks went by, and I was asked by the Senator to join him for a private drink at his apartment at the United Nations Plaza. Our appointment was set for 5 P.M. I arrived a couple of minutes early, and promptly at 5 his secretary entered the lobby, saw me, walked over, and said, "The Senator will be a few moments late. Would you care to come up to the apartment and wait?" We went upstairs, and she let me in. She invited me to make myself a drink and left me alone as she returned to work. I wandered about the living room, looking at the JFK memorabilia. Cigarette boxes, pictures, mementos—it gave me chills.

The Senator arrived. We chatted for half an hour, and I then apologized, explaining that I had to attend a screening. He asked, "What's a screening?" I thought he was kidding, but he was serious. I explained that a screening was held by movie companies to show those in the media a film about to be released, to give them ample time to write reviews or make comment about the picture when it was released. He asked the name of the film. I said, *Lord Love a Duck*. He looked at me as though I'd made up the title. I explained that I knew nothing of the film, but that a writer friend of mine had produced this picture (or directed it—I cannot remember now). His name was George Axelrod. He had a fine track record in his own ball park, and he was to be my guest that night, and I had to see the film in order to interview him.

I later entered the screening room, a long projection room which, unlike a general-admission theater, has an entrance door at each side of the screen. I found myself a seat in the center of the house. It was almost filled, and I was sitting directly in front of Axelrod and directly behind the screenwriter. The picture started. Five minutes went by and I knew it was going to be murder on my ass, for it was very bad. I had to sit there. I didn't have the guts to leave, with the people who had made the film all around me.

At that moment, the door to the left of the screen opened, and in the backlight you could see that it was Senator Kennedy and Bill vanden Heuvel peering into the darkened projection room. He had called my home, and my daughter had given him the address of the screening room. They entered, and as their eyes adjusted to the dark, there was buzzing—"Bob Kennedy just walked in!" He walked from row one upward, peering into each row. He finally saw me, and people moved over to make room for the Senator and vanden Heuvel.

They sat there for about three minutes, and he must have been a very quick study, for he turned to me and quite audibly asked, "What's this about?" I mumbled something (remember Axelrod behind me), and it seemed to hold him still for a moment, and then after another minute he turned again, and asked, "When are we leaving?"

Well! The Senator's wish is the Senator's command. I was grateful for the out; I could now blame my departure on him. We and our wives left, and walked a couple of blocks to Lindy's.

I have never seen such public recognition of anyone as RFK received in just those two blocks. I was reminded of walking down the street once with Sidney Poitier after he had won his Academy Award. We were stopped every three feet by someone who wanted to shake his hand, request an autograph, or compliment him. I properly was totally ignored. Finally, one little old lady rushed up, turned her back to Sidney, and said, "Barry, darling, I listen to your program every night! Every night! I go to bed with you every night! But every night! Thank you!" I thanked her, and Sidney and I walked a few feet, and I mumbled to him, "Drop dead!" But the kind of recognition that came to Kennedy on the streets of New York —from cabbies, news dealers, passersby, simply everyone —was absolutely overwhelming. Again, they felt he was theirs, and he represented them!

Kennedy had never been in Lindy's before, and he was fascinated. The waiters came scurrying. As we sat there over Danish and coffee, a little girl approached me with a menu and asked for my autograph. I motioned at Kennedy and said, "Don't you want his?" She shook her head from side to side. I signed it, and said to Bob, "She isn't old enough to vote anyway." A minute later, a lady came back with the menu, fire in her eyes, and yelled at me, "She doesn't want your autograph! She wants *his!*"—

pointing at the Senator. So much for settling my hash. Kennedy just looked at me and smirked. I'm sorry, but smirked is the only word for it.

I did not see him again until the tragedy that befell Martin Luther King. When I heard the news of King's murder, I immediately called Sidney Poitier and asked if I could attend the funeral with him. He told me that he was making other arrangements for himself, Harry Belafonte, and Bill Cosby, but he was sending friends on a private jet to Atlanta and he would include me on that manifest. I flew to Atlanta from New York's Marine Air Terminal with Sammy Davis, Jr.; theatrical producer Hillard Elkins; singer Nancy Wilson; her accompanist; and Robert Culp. It was a solemn trip, with Sammy occupying himself doing fast draws with his side arm. I asked him why he carried a gun. He sat across the tiny aisle of the six-passenger jet and said, "Well, I get a lotta bad mail. Married to Mai [Britt], and ya never know when you're gonna need it." I asked if he'd ever seen the results of a professional beating. He said no. I told him that while he was *reaching* for his weapon, if there was a professional contract out on him, the hoods would have had both his legs broken, given him a brain concussion, and left him for dead with his gun still half out of the holster. My final advice: "If you feel the need—get a professional bodyguard." And he did.

We arrived in Atlanta, and rooms were at a premium; strangers were being assigned to room with each other. I drew for my roomie Sammy's press aide, who'd flown in from L.A. We met in Sammy's suite, where Sammy immediately picked up the phone, imperiously called room service, and ordered $500 worth of soul food. Do you have any idea of how large a quantity that is, and what it looks like? Having been raised in a Mexican neighborhood didn't help me a bit. His suite at the Regency Hyatt House, a brand-new addition then to the Atlanta skyline, was a madhouse. Performers, politicians, local leaders, high-yellow girls (all carrying small white poodles, and all moving about on marvelously shaped legs), while the phone never stopped. I went to my room. I called Sidney Poitier at his hotel; we made a date for dinner that night, and I was asked to stop by his suite first. After I'd changed and as I was starting to leave the room, my roommate walked in and took over his bed to unpack his things.

At Poitier's suite Bill Cosby gave me a warm hello, and we all went to dinner. Alan King was at the next table, and with us were Diahann Carroll and on my left a man who'd been introduced, but whose name hadn't registered. So over soup I turned to him and said, "I'm sorry—I didn't get your name." He said, "Berry Gordy." I then asked the largest shaper of musical tastes in America, the founder and guiding brain of Motown Music, "What do you do for a living?" He looked at me oddly, and said, "I'm in the music business." The rest of the table overheard it, and roared. A minute or two later, with an angelic look on his face, Gordy turned to me and asked, "What do you do for a living?"

After dinner, Alan King took me aside and said that Senator Kennedy was holding a meeting upstairs for certain members of the media, some of the black entertainers, and the local members of Dr. King's organization. When we got there, we were greeted by the Senator, Mrs. Kennedy, and Bill vanden Heuvel, who sat on the floor and made notes of what was being said. Barbara McNair was there, and so were Eartha Kitt, Sammy Davis, Jr., and a great many people who had a lot to say about civil rights.

The only white man to whom the blacks addressed themselves, and properly, was Bob Kennedy, who'd come country miles from a Sunday, years before, when he'd convened a black group in New York to find out about the black experience, and according to them, had shown himself so naive that they'd left disheartened, and disgusted at his ignorance of their problem. Now, almost at the moment he was handed the news of King's death while he was on the road campaigning, he had delivered the most moving speech recorded by anyone about what King's loss would mean to America, and how he, Robert Kennedy, could understand assassination better, and feel its tragic effects more deeply, than anyone else. So now the blacks *knew* him, and trusted him, and loved him.

The meeting broke up, and Bob and Ethel said good night and "See you in the morning." I went to my room and found a doorknob card which asked that I order my breakfast by checking off the items I wished and the time I wanted them delivered. I left a 7 A.M. call. My roommate was still out. I fell asleep.

The next thing I knew, he was shaking me awake, and he said, "It's seven thirty—you better get up." I showered and shaved quickly, and as I rubbed myself dry, he said, "Boy! this is a great hotel. At seven o'clock the doorbell rang and a waiter brought me orange juice, two eggs over easy, bacon, an English muffin, and coffee!" I growled, "You ate *my* breakfast!" I had to rush, without even juice or coffee, to Harry Belafonte's quarters, where marching instructions were being issued. He was in complete charge, and handled himself like a field commander.

It was a terribly hot day in Atlanta, and thousands, tens of thousands, marched the miles to the cemetery. As we began our march, in that scorching heat, doors of homes owned by whites were closed, but as we walked on, some dropping from heat prostration, we moved into the poorer, black, area of Atlanta. Chairs were brought out to the curbs, and pitchers of cold water were proffered. There is little to be said about who was there. It's all been done. But I have never seen a greater outpouring of love and respect and honor accorded to one man, save in the funeral procession of John Kennedy.

When we reached the plain of Morehouse College, we found it a sea of humanity. Bodies crushed tightly against one another, and there, some 50 feet away, were Senator and Mrs. Kennedy, being pushed along by the wave. He raised a hand as he saw me. Behind me, a CBS man with a microphone saw the recognition and asked me if I could get him an interview with the Senator. I waved at Bob and gestured to the mike held by the CBS reporter, and Bob shook his head—no.

But the surging mass was pushing us closer together, and in minutes we were shoulder to shoulder. Someone on the speakers' dais saw the Kennedys and asked the mob to push them forward so that they might be there. I was pushed along with them. The three of us mounted the speakers' platform. A Georgia state trooper saw me, decided instantly I didn't belong there, opened a back door behind the platform, and shoved me through it.

I was standing, alone, on a deserted dirt road. I walked about half a mile. Hot, jacket off, tie off, shirt open, running sweat, and I saw Peter Lawford and his manager, Milt Ebbins, trying to thumb a ride. A couple stopped and asked, "Aren't you Peter Lawford?" He said, "Yes— can you give us a ride to the Hyatt Hotel?" They opened the door, and off we rode. On arrival I went straight to the bar for the longest, coolest drink I can recall. I went upstairs to pack and await the departure of the jet back to New York.

On April 24, 1968, I received the following letter:

Dear Barry,

I am sorry we had to meet under such sad circumstances, but I hope we will have another opportunity to get together in the coming weeks. In any event, I wanted you to know how nice it was to see you.

With best regards,

Sincerely,
Bob
Robert F. Kennedy

The Kennedy campaign took him west to Oregon and defeat, and California and victory. By the time his victory in California had reached the East Coast I had long since finished my broadcast, come home, and put on pajamas and robe, and I sat and watched the California proceedings in my den. The Kennedy speech was over, it was on to Chicago, and the network men were beginning to wrap it up. The crawl on the screen (credits of director, cameramen, etcetera) had started when I saw frenetic activity by the newsmen behind the crawl. The credits went off the screen, and the news of the shooting of Bob was announced. Mine was, like yours, an all-night vigil, as I constantly called newsrooms for more than I was getting onscreen. And then that wrenching, terrifying announcement of his death.

The next time I "saw" Senator Robert F. Kennedy was at St. Patrick's Cathedral in New York. It was the middle of the night, and teams of six honorary pallbearers stood, three on each side of the plain casket, while a seventh man pronounced the Catholic Litany for the spirit of Kennedy. His brother Ted sat in a dark corner of the church and watched most of the night. I remember standing with writer Jack Newfield, who later wrote a moving document of the life and times of Robert Kennedy, and actor-scholar-author Robert Vaughn, who joined us later for a drink. I kept remembering Bob's letter, and what he'd written—"I hope we will have another opportunity to get together in the coming weeks."

During the period when Richard and Sybil Burton's separation and divorce were on front pages worldwide, I was nothing more than an interested reader, having met Richard but once during an interview, years before, when he had briefly appeared in New York.

The Burtons were friendly with actor Stanley Baker, who had come to the program often—and still does, when he's in New York. Stanley Baker was in town to set preproduction plans with moviemaker Joseph E. Levine. I invited them to the broadcast to talk about it, and inadvertently David Susskind was invited as well. I say "inadvertently" for David had been in Hollywood attacking the studios, their films, their distribution, their moguls, their dynasties. He had not made himself popular with film people, and there was hardly a day that *Daily Variety* or the *Hollywood Reporter*, the trade dailies, did not carry another Susskind blast. He disliked Joseph E. Levine; Levine hated Susskind! Neither knew the other was going to be on the program. They were invited by my producer, and neither thought to ask, "Who else will be there?"

Susskind arrived alone, and a few moments before air time Levine arrived, with Stanley Baker and another British actor, who sat on the sidelines. This last had obviously been elbow-bending for quite some hours (if not a lifetime). They were also accompanied by a lovely silver-haired lady, who without being introduced simply took a seat in the corner. The broadcast began, and it turned out to be one of the free-for-alls of the year! Levine drew and quartered Susskind; Susskind butted and and badgered Levine. Susskind called Levine a "quick buck artist." Levine said Susskind was an ignorant idiot who hadn't made an original film in his life, who did nothing but "remakes of older, proven hits."

As it turned out, it was all being filmed, for a team of TV photographers were following Levine around doing a "day in the life of Joe," and they had no idea when they started the film rolling, at the program's beginning, that they were about to film the "fight of the century."

Stanley Baker, not a particularly reserved Briton, was nonetheless overwhelmed by the attack and counterattack, and remained mostly silent during the show. He was so intent on who was saying what to whom that he forgot to plug his picture.

The drunken companion at one point hoisted himself from his chair, stumbled to the microphone, and almost fell, but was quickly helped by the silver-haired lady, who had jumped from her chair to hold his arm and to slowly insert him into an empty chair in front of a microphone. I could hardly say, "Sir, don't speak—you're drunk!" It made no difference—for as he faced the mike, his eyes rolled expressively and dramatically in his head, and he started to say something, belched loudly on the air, and went to sleep, or passed out.

The program continued to yell itself to conclusion. At that point Levine and Susskind immediately started to talk amicably. Stanley Baker introduced me to the lady the press of the world had been looking for, in order to get her statement. He said, "Barry, may I introduce Mrs. Sybil Burton." I looked at her, looked at him—and said,

"You mean I had the news story of the world in this studio for two hours, and you didn't tell me?" They just smiled. We all repaired to El Morocco. There Levine wound up doing coin tricks for all, while I thought, What a stinkin' reporter *I* am!

Later, when Sybil opened the most chic discotheque in New York, called Arthur, we became friendly. It was opened by a syndicate of Sybil's friends, Stanley Baker among them, who pooled their funds, and for a few years was the most "in" place of New York for the "beautiful people." It was jammed nightly from opening till the wee hours, with records being played at ear-piercing levels, and the live group was led by Jordan Christopher, now married to Sybil Burton. The investors, I am told, made a lot of money—but Stanley didn't introduce me to that group either!

Each night, during the period when I worked in one saloon, a well-dressed gentleman—no, change that to *impeccably* dressed—would come in alone; sit down at a table near the dais, sometimes alone, sometimes with a friend; and pay close attention to everything that happened on "stage." This went on for months. I didn't know his name, and if I had known it, it would have meant nothing. He looked correct, moneyed, and proper. After he'd listened and watched for months, he finally came forward one night and introduced himself, and then added, "I know you're originally from Los Angeles. I'm going out there tomorrow, and if you care to, I'd like very much to call on your mother and father and tell them how well their son is doing." I thanked him for his graciousness, and gave him their address.

Two weeks passed. In the interim I called L.A., and my mother told me that a very nice man by the name of

Salvey had called on them. They had had tea and honey cake together. They'd talked for an hour or more. He had been the essence of courtesy. He had paid me nice compliments and made my folks beam with pleasure. When he returned to the saloon, he complimented me on what charming "folks" I had, and said I was very lucky. I thanked him. Shortly thereafter, he died of a heart attack on a golf course. His obituary notice contained the information that he was a major partner in one of the largest gambling syndicates in America!

Years before, in Miami Beach, the local press, reporting the activities of the Miami Crime Commission, was having a field day. There were many former members of the underworld living in the area and ostensibly engaged in legitimate business. The crime commission didn't think so. But the best it could do, with its untold funds, investigative staffs, detecting devices, and bugs, was come up with "mug shots" of what the men had looked like when arrested in Detroit, New York, or St. Louis at the ages of 19 or 21, and what they looked like now, in their 50's and 60's. Then, of course, the commission would print prominently what business they were in, where it was located, and where they lived. In some cases, the names of their children were given, and where they went to school. Talk about "the sins of the fathers"! I thought it the yellowest form of journalism. I wasn't about to protect a working crime figure, but it has always been my understanding that we must prove guilt, and assume innocence until guilt is proved. The crime commission couldn't seem to act that way. It was using the press as its tool, and the press was allowing itself to be used. I talked about it a lot on the air. It did not make friends for me with the crime commission or with the radio-station owner (who was a member), and the press didn't care too much for me either. But the radio-station owner was making a lot of money from my program, so his greed overcame his scruples, and the newspaper guys individually dropped in, and we got along fine. They blamed it all on press management.

It had a strange ending. Later, when I came to New York and Chandler's, three or four nights a week different small groups of men would drop in, order a bottle to be placed on the table, and pass the night away. I had never seen any of them. But they made no trouble; in fact, they spoke quietly among themselves. After some months, as the broadcast finished, I left the dais just as that night's group were rising to leave. I stopped to thank them for coming in. One replied, "It's our pleasure. Joe A. [Adonis] thinks you're a good kid!"

Some time later, as I was leaving the restaurant one night, one of them drove up, jumped out of his car, and seeing me, pulled me into a corner. He was perspiring, and whispered, "Be careful. I know ya been fighting with Winchell. I don't know what it's all about, but I hear there's a 'small' contract out on ya!" I was careful for about two weeks. Then I dropped my guard. Shortly thereafter, I found myself awakening on a sidewalk after a slugging. I guess I should have been careful longer.

Finished with saloons, I now went back into the studio, and Eleanor Roosevelt, keeping her word to me, came to be interviewed. She was a delight. As we spoke, I could look over her shoulder at the control room, and as I glanced up, Jerry Lewis walked in, surrounded by an entourage of about eight. Eleanor Roosevelt had come to the studio *alone*.

When her discussion was concluded, Lewis and company trooped into the studio, and as they stood in line I asked Mrs. Roosevelt if I might introduce my friends. She said, "Of course." I then proceeded with the introductions, and I said, "This is Mr. Jerry Lewis." She shook hands, smiled, and said, "Mr. Lewis," and continued to the next introduction, without a sign of recognition for one of the world's best-known comedians.

I then asked if I might see her downstairs (from the fourth floor) to get her to her car. I assumed she had a limousine. She replied, "Oh no, I'll just jump into a cab." I insisted on seeing her to the street, asked my guests to wait a minute, and went with her to Broadway, which then still had two-way traffic. She saw a cab heading uptown across the street. She whistled, yelled, "Taxi!," smiled, waved at me, ran across the street, jumped in, and threw me another smile as the cab pulled away. I thought of the showy entourage upstairs against the marvelous humility I'd just witnessed.

I recalled, too, the night that Sammy Davis, Jr., had come to the studio with his entourage, a large one, and one of them carried a big black suitcase. He placed the bag on a desk in the rear of the studio, opened it, carefully mixed a Scotch and water (it was a portable bar!), and handed it to Sammy, who was lounging across the mike from me. He didn't ask whether anyone else cared for anything (a Tab?), and our interview began. Ah! the rich! Or the time Eddie Fisher came to the studio with sixteen in his party! I counted them! Whenever he reached for anything—a cigarette, ashtray, anything— someone beat him to it. Of such things is bankruptcy born.

Eddie—who had begun his climb to stardom at the old Riviera nightclub in Fort Lee, New Jersey, when he stepped in for the star, who had a cold—was introduced to me by his manager, Milton Blackstone, who said,

"Barry, he's going to be a big star." I said, "I know; I was there that night." Milton continued, "Tell him how to save his money." And I told Milton, "Boy, have you got the wrong number!"

Dick Gregory, an impassioned man, came to the broadcast whenever he was in New York, and he, like all of us, was demolished, crushed, stunned by the JFK assassination. A long time went by while Gregory conducted his own investigation. He traveled a lot. He asked many questions. He filled a dossier. He was convinced it had been the plot of more than one demented man.

He came on the air and spoke for two hours. When the show was over, he said, "Man, you come to my hotel, one block away, and I'll show you some stuff that'll scare the shit outta ya. They wanta take over this country, and just about the first thing they wanta do is kill this nigger!"

I went with him. His room was on the thirtieth floor of a midtown hotel. A very small room, with a large, open window two feet from his bed, upon which we sat as he showed me his dossier. There was only one small chair in the room, but there was that big, open window. I suffer from fear of heights. Not airplanes, just open places. And he kept repeating, "They're gonna kill this nigger!" And I kept looking at that big, open window. And every time he said it, I thought the door would be flung open and four guys in sheets would yell, "There he is, and get that skinny son-of-a-bitch too—we don't want any witnesses!"

A couple of nights later, the late Preston Sturges came by. He was a director who'd made a wide reputation in Hollywood. Five minutes before the program he asked, "Do you have a drink in the joint?" I didn't, but a friendly shop nearby would rush a fifth of Scotch over.

We were on the air when the Scotch arrived. The producer opened the bottle and put it at his elbow along with some paper cups. He had one, straight, then another, then another, and for two hours gave me one of the most lucid discussions of moviemaking I'd ever heard. When the show was over, there was one drink, barely, left in the fifth. He looked down and said, "Well, no need for this to go to waste." He poured it into a cup, threw it back, said good night, and walked steadily from the studio. He had consumed a full fifth of Scotch during the broadcast, without a tremor, or a thick tongue, or a misplaced word.

He died soon thereafter, but I have no reason to think liquor had anything to do with it.

Telephone talk shows are common throughout the country today. The phenomenon started by accident. Back in the WOR all-night days, when I was tentatively trying to stick my tongue into the talk-through-the-night format rather than play the prescribed records, the studio light went on that let me know a call was on the telephone for me. I addressed the microphone with "Just a moment, folks; there's some jerk on the phone" (which gives you an idea of the high level of vocabulary I was using then). I picked up the telephone, and a voice said, "Barry? The 'jerk' is Woody Herman!"

In those days, the two-way conversation was not heard. Only I could be heard. So I repeated, "Woody Herman? How are you?"—etcetera, etcetera. The call completed, there were immediately calls from listeners who wanted to know, "Was that really Woody Herman?" More and more calls, all on the air, and all of them with only my voice audible to the audience. Some of the calls were lovely. Some informative. Some gushing. Some pure invective and hate. The last type I finished off quickly with a return insult, or "Drop dead!" The listeners, not being able to hear the other side of the call, thought I was being rude. I wasn't. I was merely paying back in the currency of the moment.

When WOR fired me and I repaired to Florida and the Copa lounge, Jan Murray, suffering a back ailment, was ordered to lie flat on his back during recuperation. He was being visited by a theatrical-agent friend, and I was on the air during that visit. They were listening. I had invited another comic to come to the microphone in the lounge and "spell" me while I had a cup of coffee with a group seated below the dais. But just prior to that I had interviewed a lady who had been described to me as "an exotic dancer." Mind you, radio was not nearly so permissive in those days. The words stripper, hooker, V.D. were simply not used. "Hell" was unthinkable! The exotic dancer told me sweetly that she danced with veils, which gradually came off, until the last one. I asked, stammeringly, "And what are you left with?" And she replied, "One veil, and a flower in my belly button." Belly button? In that era on the air? Horrendous! I quickly thanked her, got rid of her, and called the comic up to say a few funny things and take some calls while I had the coffee.

Harry Morton, Jan's visitor, listening to the exchange with the exotic dancer, turned to him and said, "Watch this. I'll have him [me] saying 'belly button' a dozen times before I'm through with him." The comic, suffering back agony, pleaded, "Don't! Please don't! I'll start to laugh, and the pain will kill me!" Nonetheless, the call was made. The comic at the Copa picked up the phone.

"Hello."

"Mr. Gray?"

"No, this isn't Barry Gray, but I'm sitting in for him. May I help you?"

"Well, I didn't hear it, but I just got home, and my phone has been ringing constantly—calls from friends and neighbors who say he used my name in an insulting manner, and I'm going to sue him and the station and the club for a million dollars!"

"You're going to sue the club, the station, and Barry Gray for a million dollars?" the comic repeated.

At that a hush fell over the assembled audience. My ears pricked up.

"Why?" asked the comic.

" 'Cause my name is Sol Bellybutton!"

"Your name is Sol Bellybutton?"

This all on the air.

The visitor (caller) turned to Jan Murray in bed and whispered, "That's one."

My comic substitute at the mike:

"But Mr. Bellybutton [that's two], Barry had this young lady on the air a minute ago, and she said she wore a flower in her belly button [that's three]—that's all there was to it."

By now I had rushed back to the microphone, taken it back, picked up the telephone, and said, in my con-nest voice, "Mr. Bellybutton [that's four], I can assure you no harm was meant. It was just a simple exchange, and I had no idea that it would upset anyone. I didn't know what she was going to say, and I had no idea that anyone named Bellybutton [that's five] lived in the area"—and by now the comic at home was writhing in combined laughter and pain on the bed, and damn near fell on the floor. I "Bellybuttoned" the caller about a dozen times more in trying to calm him down. I think the words went

130

out on the air about seventeen times, and finally the caller said, "Barry? It's me, Harry Morton, you shmuck!"

I had been suckered.

But it *was* a breakthrough in radio permissiveness!

Contrast the fear of that moment over uttering the words "belly button," and leap forward many years to the time when Dr. David Reuben, author of *Everything You Always Wanted to Know About Sex*, was making the rounds, plugging his book. I believe Reuben made his first appearance with me. I had read the book (and you did too—don't lie), and I really didn't know what to do about the interview. How should I handle it? I decided to simply read the questions from the book, and let him answer them in his own way. After all, he was an established doctor and analyst. We started our talk.

Meanwhile, Basil Paterson, then a New York State Senator and now vice-chairman of the Democratic National Committee, was driving down from a session in Albany. WMCA's signal power of 5,000 watts is heard on good nights in Boston, and sometimes even in northern Florida, where we compete with a station from Cuba, but we are essentially aimed at the tristate area of New York, New Jersey, and Connecticut. Paterson, leaving Albany, with his radio set at 570 (WMCA's wavelength), fiddled with the dial. He was getting static that night. He was driving on the New York State Thruway, a high-speed thoroughfare which moves from north to south and bisects the state. As he drove, he continued to fool with the radio dial. Nothing but static, and then he suddenly heard Dr. Reuben's voice boom through his car speaker with the word "orgasm." At that moment, Paterson entered a tunnel on the thruway. As Paterson later put it, "I pushed the throttle to the floor and went through that tunnel at a hundred miles an hour to try to hear the end of the sentence!"

It is interesting to me, in observing the transition to American acceptance of broadcast language, that not one letter came to me complaining about Dr. Reuben's comments, and he went on, of course, to many appearances on shows like those of Johnny Carson, Merv Griffin, and Mike Douglas, not to forget *Kup's Show* in Chicago. My, did he sell a lot of books! It may all go to prove that we as a nation have good ears, but our plumbing needs an overhaul.

Most radio stations today, particularly those involved in telephone talk or interviews, have all of their programs on seven-second microdelay. That means that what you hear on your radio was actually said in the studio seven seconds earlier. If anything is said which the interviewer, or telephone-call taker, feels is obscene, he can press a button at his elbow, and it kills the call and prevents it from being aired. There is another backstop, in the control room. I am hard pressed to remember when I last used my "kill" button, but I *do* remember how we got it!

It was about three minutes before the end of a certain program. I had bidden my guests good night and thought I had some comment ready about an upcoming program, but found my dates were inaccurate and decided against making the announcement that night. So I said, "Well, time for one call." And I picked up the phone.

A male voice said, "Barry, I've been listening to you for more than ten years."

I thought, That's pretty good—he likes me.

I said, "Thank you."

He said, "You're still full of shit!"

No microdelay. It was live, that moment, on the air.

The station installed the new delay equipment at once. But the installer had to step over the body of an engineer hysterically laughing on the floor.

As I wrote the word "body" a moment ago, I was reminded of a hot, humid, oppressive night in New York when the studio air conditioning performed naturally and broke down. We decided to broadcast from the boss's office, which was individually air-conditioned and was practically soundproof against street noises. I was interviewing a national labor leader about strike strife in New York. The cab drivers wanted more money and a better pension plan, and their tactic was to drive about New York, failing to pick up passengers, but hooting horns and demonstrating.

I thanked him after half an hour, and he left the office/studio. I walked him to the elevator and said good night. I had a five-minute break while the news was on the air. My producer came rushing down the hall and, ashen-faced, said, "You'd better come into the office. I think something's wrong with the engineer." I ran in. He lay prostrate on the floor. I felt for his pulse. There was none. I called the Rescue Squad of the New York City Police Department, which was located right around the corner. The squad arrived in an instant, but he was dead, of a massive coronary.

We had to wait for the New York County Medical Examiner to arrive to make it official, for he had died without a doctor in attendance, and it was required under New York law for the medical examiner to pronounce death and then remove the body for an autopsy. I had two guests waiting—Alexander H. Cohen, the Broadway and London producer, who also produces the ABC *Tony Awards* show each year, and Joel Schenker, another Broadway producer, who had brought the late Van Heflin to Broadway in a brilliant play, *A Case of Libel*, and introduced Stacey Keach to his first great success in *Indians*. I quickly explained to them what had happened. They understood. They went into a small, un-air-conditioned studio, and talked to each other on the air about Broadway, the theater, and personalities, explaining that I would be along in a few moments. I was at the telephone outside, calling a station executive. I was told not to call the engineer's widow—the station owner would take care of that. It was the grimmest broadcast I can remember, but Cohen and Schenker, in the tradition of their calling, "made the show go on."

Rex Reed, the motion-picture critic and now critic at large for the New York Daily News Syndicate, but then of *The New York Times*, startled me the most before we had our delay system installed. The subject matter that night was "Censorship—in Newsprint and the Media." Along with Rex, I had invited Judith Crist, then of the *Today* show; Hollis Alpert, managing editor of *Saturday Review–World* magazine and regular contributor to *Playboy* magazine; and Liz Smith, motion-picture critic for *Cosmopolitan* magazine.

We had meandered along for a while with stories of censorship and implied censorship, and had exchanged various opinions, when Rex Reed said, "I know there's censorship at *The New York Times*. I interviewed George Peppard in his suite at the Plaza a few days ago, and every other word out of his mouth was 'shit.' *The New York Times* changed every 'shit' to 'crap'!" Well, we were on the air, and the earliest lesson you learn in radio is, when a gaffe like that is made, keep going; your audience will never believe they heard it! We kept going.

I remember once working in front of a packed audience as the broadcast was under way, and I asked a guest why he wasn't liked by a friend of mine. And he simply replied, "Fuck him." I looked at the audience. They *looked* the same, and I continued with the interview. When it was over, I told the guest what he'd said. He said, "I can't believe it!" We went into the control room and rolled back the tape. There was the expletive. Clean, pure, pristine, and expressive. The people in the audience *must* have heard it. But they didn't believe they had. It sounded like it, they thought. But he couldn't have. He had.

One time the mayor of New York City was trying to establish, through public referendum, a review board of the New York City Police, aptly dubbed "New York's finest." Charges of brutality, corruption, and venality had been leveled against some members of the force. And the department and the courts, through investigating committees, had collared the culprits, removed them from the force, and in some cases prosecuted and jailed them. But I was and am against a *civilian* group policing the police, for it could easily be a catchall for crackpot complaints and misguided anger against the cop on the beat, instead of fury leveled against an administration that allows our crowded, stifled community to be poorly housed, badly fed, unemployed, and allowed to see its "elected" representatives only at election time. (Most of the poor don't vote; they don't believe in the system—and more and more citizens in the middle-income class are beginning to share their cynicism.)

The late Jackie Robinson, while a life-insurance executive, hearing of my opposition to the review board, sent me the following letter:

Dear Barry:

Last Thursday I heard for the first time that you had consented to be one of the three co-chairmen aiding the PBA [Patrolmen's Benevolent Association] fight against the civilian review board. I told my informer I did not believe the information was true. "I know Barry to be a true liberal in the purest sense of the word," I insisted.

I hope I am right, Barry. For, in my opinion only the bigots and those who have something to hide are afraid of a civilian review board. All the excuses given by Mr. Cassese [formerly head of the PBA] and his ilk seem to form a smokescreen to camouflage their own personal prejudices.

It is difficult for me to believe that you would be a party to this deception. For so many years you have advocated so many positions which you now appear to repudiate. You have aligned yourself with the Bill Buckley types and others who are as capable of seeking to eliminate persons of your religion as fast as they would eliminate persons of my race.

If it is true that you have accepted leadership in this fight against the civilian review board—and in the passing days there has been no indication that you have not—I must refuse, in the future, to have anything to do with your program. I would hope other Negroes would feel the same way. That is why I have sent copies of this letter to persons whose names are herewith listed. I hope I am wrong, Barry. I could not in good conscience call you a bigot. But you know the logical conclusion about the man who lies down with hogs. The hogs do not end up smelling like men. The concept of you and Bill Buckley fighting shoulder to shoulder would be ludicrous if it were not tragic. I can understand Buckley, Barry. I cannot understand you.

Sincerely,
Jackie
Jackie Robinson

Encl.

The "enclosure":

Copies of my letter to you have been sent to the following:
Mr. Harry Belafonte
Mr. Sammy Davis, Jr.
Mr. Jim Smith, assistant to Mayor Lindsay
Rev. Wyatt Tee Walker [Dr. Martin Luther King's special counsel]
Rev. George Lawrence
Mr. Floyd McKissick, executive director, CORE
Mr. Stokely Carmichael, SNCC
Mr. Roy Wilkins, executive director, NAACP
Mr. Jack Greenberg, director-counsel, NAACP legal
Dr. Martin Luther King, Jr.
A. Philip Randolph
James Baldwin
Whitney Young, Urban League
James Meredith
Ted Poston, *New York Post*
James Hicks, executive editor, *Amsterdam News*
Mr. Jesse Walker, managing editor, *Amsterdam News*

I read and reread the letter openmouthed. I had known Jackie for more than twenty years. I could not believe the letter's contents, but much more than that, I could not believe Jackie had chosen to send it, in the same mail, to the most influential black men of our society, in almost every case friends of mine, who had, over the years, appeared with me often, on WMCA microphones, to expound their views on America's terrible treatment of the black minority.

I had come full circle. From being ostracized for defending Bill Robinson's right to appear in any nightclub that chose to hire him, for defending Josephine Baker's right to dine in any restaurant, I was now being maligned by Jackie Robinson for opposing what I considered a cheap political ploy by the local politicos to get the heat off them because they were not doing *their* job! What the hell did that have to do with the police? I telephoned Jackie. Not in. I telephoned again, leaving my name each time. Not in. Finally, I wrote:

My dear Jackie:
I have called your office twice since I received your letter of August 17th, with no reply from you. My calls have been made in order to tell you how surprised I was by the contents of that letter, for my views regarding Mayor John Lindsay's proposed Civilian Review Board, reviewing Police Actions, have been public since his campaign for election. I told him then, publicly, on the air, that it was the only issue on which we parted company, but I supported him in spite of it. I felt then, as I feel now, that the board is a phoney panacea for what the true evils of our society are, namely: poor housing, unemployment, and a lack of equal opportunity for all. The anger and outrage caused by these inequalities bring many members of the minorities to grips with the only visible members of the establishment, the police officer, and their rage is often vent on him, whether he be white or black.

Early in the radio business I covered a police beat, and I would suggest, respectfully, that my credentials in this area are far better than Algernon Black [member of the Lindsay Committee for the Review Board], or the mayor's, or yours. I am, and have been for years against *community* brutality and would help establish, in an instant, a review board for that. And bring to justice all the venal, the gougers, the dishonest, regardless of their position, politically, or economically, or their race, or faith.

About Buckley: I am reminded by your criticism of the time I supported FDR, and was told the "Communists supported him too." I said then, "I'm sorry for that—but he's still the most qualified, better than [Herbert] Hoover (and then Landon), and I will vote for him, and hope he can keep the Reds at bay." I must add: I was against the Review Board plan long before Buckley made a public statement on the subject. I have never spoken with him about it, and had no idea, until it was made public, that the Conservatives agreed *with my position*. But then, so do lots of Liberals (ask them) and people of all political persuasions. It was nothing to do with their attitudes toward minorities— it *does* have to do with their support (and mine) of a strong, moralized Police Department, which without public support, and demoralized, would make New York, in fact, an asphalt jungle.

You say in your letter, that you cannot, "in good conscience" call me a "bigot." I would hope not Jackie, for my credentials in the field of human understanding are rather extensive, beginning with my breakthrough for Negro entertainment, in the then lily-white areas of Miami Beach in 1948 (The Step Brothers), my bringing the late Bill Robinson into an all-white cub (the Copa) through a police guard, and then having the club burned down around me by the Klan because of refusal to knuckle under to their threats. And my loss of a television career, two physical beatings, and an estimated two million dollar loss in billing, when I undertook to bring the Josephine Baker–Stork Club story to the listening public. During that period most of my liberal friends ran, most of my Negro friends ran, and Josephine Baker ran. You may call me foolish, but never, never, bigoted.

Nothing however, including my disappointment in people, during that era, has changed my views about the black man's plight. I believed in "Black Power" (economic and political) long before Messrs. Carmichael and McKissick gave it a name, and have exhorted the audience often to pursue these themes. I intend to continue, for these are the real issues of the 60's and the future, and when these are fully developed we won't need the spurious issue of a Review Board to keep the minorities happy with pap, while they suffer the pangs of hunger, the filth of improper housing, and the injustice of unemployment due to illiteracy, lack of job training, and the denial of jobs within our labor force in New York.

But the greatest disappointment I have in your letter, Jackie, is based on our long, long, friendship, and I would welcome your views at any time and on any issue. But to send a copy of your letter to some distinguished Americans, some of whom are my friends, before you had a chance to hear my reply, is a form of Kangaroo Court, and constitutes, in its threat of boycott, implied blackmail. If you had come to me, or called, and discussed our differences on the issue, and I felt your arguments surpassed mine, I would easily have moved to your side of the aisle, and said "if it means that much to you, Jackie, I will fight with you." But by saying to me, as you have in your letter, "you must agree or I will boycott you, and see to it that other prominent men do the same," you give me little chance, as a man, but to hold fast my view, and sadly, to measure you by your letter.

Sincerely,
Barry Gray

Two weeks later I received an answer from Jackie, in much the same tone as his first, and completely ignoring my charges relating to his mailing copies of his letter to respected men in the field of civil liberties before I had had a chance to reply.

I found out later that one day after his letter to me was posted, and before I had received it, Mr. William Booth, then chairman of the Commission on Human Rights for the city and a frequent guest on my program, asked that a meeting be set up with Peter Straus, WMCA's owner. Booth had written a letter which read, in part, "Mr. Jackie Robinson and A. Philip Randolph join me in requesting an appointment to meet with you with reference to the Barry Gray radio shows."

The meeting was held. I was told that pressure was being brought to bear to remove me from WMCA's air. The tactic, obviously, didn't work. I never heard from Jackie again. And tragically, now I never will, in this life. But I thought, wryly, of how much alike zealots are in their tactics. Joseph McCarthy used the same ammunition. And so did Winchell. Unlike them, Jackie Robinson was a good man, but in this case he was a zealot.

P.S.: The Civilian Review Board was disastrously defeated at the polls.

Which brings me to William Kunstler. The firebrand attorney has been my guest, over the years, perhaps as many as a hundred times. His exposures have taken many forms, ranging from a civil-libertarian point of view to his defense of the late Congressman Adam Clayton Powell. His most recent appearance was to discuss the Middle Eastern "Yom Kippur" war and to express a pro-Arab point of view. I disagree with that position totally, and have so stated over and over since the outbreak of original hostilities going back to the Irgun and Haganah (Israel's initial and, later, official fighting force). But over the years a spokesman for the Arab League, a turncoat Jew, or a public official has joined the controversy.

The night that Kunstler appeared, I expected his statements, for he does represent the black groups, who for some unfathomable reason are anti-Israel. This is in spite of the fact that Israel has been highly visible in aid programs to the underdeveloped nations of Africa and exchange programs of students, with many blacks attending its institutions of higher learning. Furthermore, in the United States, the Jewish groups, from elders to the youth, have been alongside the blacks in every issue involving the black since American history started its long-play recording. Don't forget that slavery has long been operated and advanced by Arab groups. So, it's a "puzzlement." It has also angered, understandably, many Jews throughout the world, who in every case have given their money, and in some cases their lives, in the black cause. And "anger," as Kunstler pointed out that night, is "emotion," and "emotion takes unreasonable forms."

What happened as his words unfolded over the air was, in the first instance, that the WMCA switchboard was swamped with calls. Angry, obscene, vicious calls. Some aimed at my guest, many aimed at me. "The hell with free speech—get that bastard off the air!"

Earlier that day I had met with a new sponsor, and he had then sat in while I did some recording for a later program. He told me more than a dozen times how much he loved the program and that he rarely missed a night. How strongly he felt about the right of the different points of view to be aired. His commercial was to begin the following Monday, four days later. He left the studio, and Kunstler was on that night. Late the following afternoon, the sponsor sent me a weaseling letter. He pointed out that his business depended on public support. He was therefore canceling. So much for his love of free speech.

Other people disappoint me sometimes for different reasons. Some years ago, the late John Aaron and Jesse Zousmer, who had produced Ed Murrow's Person to Person programs, approached me and asked if I'd like to do a pilot half hour for ABC Television, patterned after the old Murrow shows. I said I would be "honored."

Murrow used to sneak into the back of Chandler's, and listen for an hour or two, fairly often. We had a nodding acquaintance, and spent an evening together, quite by accident, when the first year of broadcast award-giving was taking place. Murrow received an award for his national programs devoted to issues in the "public interest." My award was for local programming of a like nature,

and we shared a table. His speech was unique. I can para-
phrase part of it. He said that without his microphone,
and the men who made that mike possible, he would be
just another guy at the end of the bar, growling into his
beer. I agreed totally, as I do now.

Aaron, Zousmer, and I met quite often during the
planning stage of the pilot. We were now into the last
days before the test run. I received a call from Aaron.
There would be no pilot for ABC. James Hagerty, the
network's news director and onetime press secretary to
President Eisenhower, had complained bitterly about the
test. If they did it, Aaron reported, Hagerty was "going
to walk."

I had never met Mr. Hagerty. Or his late boss, the
President. I do remember my many comments about
Eisenhower's reign as our chief executive. His stupid conduct during another Middle Eastern war; his comments,
when General of the Army, before a Senate committee,
urging nonintegration of the Armed Forces. He struck
me as a great soldier and a poor President. He constantly
gave the impression of having been briefed on every subject and not having paid too much attention, and the
briefings had obviously been very brief. He acted cravenly
during the McCarthy period, when he allowed to go un-
answered attacks on General George C. Marshall, a remarkable soldier, statesman, and Secretary of State. I
guess Hagerty remembered my comments too.

Another member of the Murrow family was yet to be
heard from, Fred Friendly. He had produced Ed Murrow's programs, and had now written a very good book
about him. When his publishers contacted me to ask if
he might appear to talk about Murrow, the book, and
himself, I was delighted to acquiesce.

On occasions when the guest is unusually well known,

or vocal enough to carry a program by himself, I invite no other guests, but prefer to talk on a one-to-one (or head-to-head, as we call it) basis with the individual. There are few who can carry a full two hours of radio, but Fred Friendly, filled with Murrow reminiscences, would certainly be one of them.

He arrived. We exchanged greetings. I told him of my tremendous regard for his deceased partner. The broadcast began. He was fine, just fine. Expansive, detailed, informative—and then the studio door swung open, and there stood motion-picture star George Peppard and his then wife, Elizabeth Ashley. Friendly looked over his shoulder at the door behind his right side, and I waved them "Hello"—and gestured that they take seats at the side of the studio. They did.

We broke for five minutes of news. And in that brief hiatus, when the mikes were dead and the news was coming from another studio, I introduced all parties, and Peppard explained to us that in driving around he had heard Friendly's introduction on the air and, being a great fan of his, wanted to take the opportunity of coming up to be introduced. Friendly was pleased, and so was I.

I had met Peppard early in his career. Our paths had crossed often. During his making of *The Victors*, we had seen each other in Rome. I had flown to London when the film had its world premiere and interviewed the entire cast as we sat, on a rain-drenched day, in the lobby of the Dorchester Hotel in the West End. We met again, as dinner partners, when he was making *The Blue Max* in Ireland and was getting up before dawn daily, learning to fly for his role in the film. And I remember that early dinner, for we finished dining about 7 to enable him to get some sleep before having to be up in time for flying.

He regaled us with funny stories about the Irish farmers being upset and calling the police, for they had seen "Nazis on the roads outside of town!" They *had* seen "Nazis," but they were Irish soldiers wearing the gray-green of the German troops, playing roles in *The Blue Max*, which dealt with a German pilot's view of the war. And Ireland, because of its unfrequented skies and great vistas of green, was perfect for the location of the film.

Back in the studio, the news ending, Peppard took his seat on the side of the room again. I reintroduced Friendly, and our exchange continued. About five minutes went by. Peppard got up, slid into a chair with a microphone in front of it, and asked Friendly if he could pose a question. I interrupted, explaining why Peppard was there, and how we'd chatted during the news. Friendly became red-faced and furious. He accused me of having invited him to be interviewed alone and then having "brought a ringer into the program!" I assured him that Peppard's appearance was purely accidental, but welcome, for he was a fine, thinking individual, and I was sure he could make a real contribution to the program. Friendly would not be assuaged, nor turned aside. He was being "set up!," "used!"—and he stormed out of the studio. To this day I've not the slightest notion what the up-to-that-point-splendid guest thought he was being set up for.

When Arthur Goldberg, former U.S. Supreme Court Justice, former U.S. Ambassador to the United Nations, and one of America's most distinguished labor negotiators, was silly enough to enter the race for the office of Governor of New York, he made gaffe after gaffe. He called Poughkeepsie (pronounced Po-kipsy) "Puff-kipsy," which proved he hadn't been around a local corner in a long time. When asked how he preferred to be addressed, he said, " 'Mr. Ambassador' will do." And when he came to my program, and spoke in a monotone for forty-five minutes, he finished by saying, "That's the longest interview I have ever granted!" I wanted to kiss his ring—but he and his entourage had gone. Gone into political anonymity, after the race was run.

Contrast that with the wit and good humor of a very famous lady, once almost a total unknown, plugging a film called *High Noon*. Its major star was, of course, Gary Cooper. The unknown, but beautiful, blond lady was Grace Kelly. Who could see into the future? That future, which is now long past, made her a princess, the mother of beautiful children, and a world-renowned celebrity.

Princess Grace came to New York for a brief stopover. Nothing daunts my producer. He called her for an interview. He had more gall than I had. The phone in her room was answered sweetly: "Hello?"

"Is Princess Grace there?"

"This is she. Who is calling, please?"

"This is the producer of the Barry Gray program on WMCA, and I wonder if you would be a guest on the program during your stay here."

"Oh—I *am* sorry, but we're leaving tonight. But how is Barry?"

"Oh, he's fine, thank you."

"I am delighted. Be sure and give him my best wishes, and tell him I hope we see him soon."

I've been to Monaco since. What do you do? Ring the bell at the palace? But that lady would have had a helluva career in films, or in Philadelphia politics. Not that she's doing badly in Monaco.

•   •

But then, I've made a few silly telephone calls myself. Like the night the world awaited the new arrival at Buckingham Palace. The Queen was about to deliver a child in the official residence, and Great Britain and the world waited as the royal obstetrical team set up the delivery room. In New York, it was a quiet night. The guests had gone. I had a few minutes to kill before I said good night, so I picked up the phone and asked the overseas operator to get me "Buckingham Palace in London."

A half minute went by, and a very British, very official voice on the other end of the line announced himself as "the press secretary at Buckingham Palace." I identified myself, and then asked, "How's the Queen doing?"

The voice replied, in regal tones, "We have nothing to report on the Queen's condition." As he started to hang up, I heard him mutter (and so did the audience), "the silly bahstahd!" Well, we were the first to know she *hadn't* had a baby—at that moment.

I went off the air for the night. Well, how many people do you know who've *talked* with someone at Buckingham Palace?

Not all have been as gracious as the press officer at Buckingham Palace. Take Jane Fonda. Or please don't take her. It started with dinner at Luchow's in New York—famous for German food, and a hangout of theatrical people on Sunday night. I was being taken to dinner by a very old friend, my former agent and then head of ABC Films in Hollwood, Martin Baum. A unit of his company was in production with *They Shoot Horses, Don't They?* Its plot had to do with the marathon-dancing period, in the Depression-ridden early thirties in Los Angeles. I had lived through it all as a youngster.

Marty and I started to discuss the period, and I told him of what I'd seen then firsthand, on the old Lick Pier, which jutted out into the Pacific, when thousands of onlookers would crowd the dance hall to watch the near-dead dancers marathoning until they dropped. The dancers hoped to pick up a few dollars, if they didn't drop. It was a Roman circus, with patrons egging the dancers on, and the dancers giving their lives, in some cases, during the contest. Marty enthusiastically suggested my doing a short-subject trailer, which would be used on ABC Television following its "night at the movies" to plug the upcoming national release of the film. I agreed.

A week later, I flew to the Coast and met with a small film crew at Lick Pier. I spent a forenoon taking the camera through the old pier, describing what it had been like—the noise, the clamor, the pitchmen, the dancers, and the degradation of the period. We wrapped up the filming about noon. As we put the equipment into the truck, two female sunbathers were lolling below us sans tops, taking the California rays. I thought how different the area had become in a generation.

We then went to the studio to do an interview with the cast, which was being directed by Sydney Pollack. It was lunchtime, or almost, and the cast would be taking a meal break. On the way, the ABC aide assigned to me suggested we stop at a fashionable men's store and look over the latest Southern California sportswear. I bought nothing but a kerchief, with a ring that held it in place around the neck.

When we arrived at the studio I greeted Jane Fonda, who had been on the air with me in New York many times, and she commented, "What a nice ring on your kerchief!" I took it off and gave it to her, and said, "Now we're married." She thanked me, and tooled the ring in her fingers. She asked, "How's everything going?" I replied, "Just fine!" She then asked, "How's your son doing? The one who was interested in space?" I told her that Michael was then First Captain (the highest-ranking cadet) at Valley Forge Military Academy in Wayne, Pennsylvania, and after graduation in June would go on to U.S.C. for a major in Aerospace Engineering, with the hope of getting an assignment to NASA.

Jane said, "With what's going on in Vietnam?" I tried to point out that the military had a great deal at stake for American interests other than Vietnam, and that my son had dreamed of a NASA assignment since Sputnik had been blasted off, when he was aged 10. He, in fact, hoped for a service career. With that, she took the ring which I had just given her and threw it right in my face.

The ABC aide was mortified. He said, "That's the rudest thing I have ever seen." I replied, "No, that's Jane Fonda. Unfortunately, her father's manner was not passed on genetically." We've not spoken since.

Back in New York, WMCA had contracted to broadcast the baseball games of the New York Yankees. That was fine, for it gave us a new, untapped audience, except that once in a while—too often—a night game would be tied up, and my guests, who had been invited to appear in time for a 10:05 P.M. program, had to wait until the game was over.

It was a bore, until the night Raquel Welch appeared. She'd been on before, and we had a marvelous exchange. She is bright, witty, informed, and a joy to talk with. But tonight she was hungry. She arrived promptly on time, waiting to be interviewed and afterward to be whisked to dinner by her escort. The game was tied. We finally got on the air at 10:50. Forty-five minutes late. But,

God! *Her* cleavage, for staring, for forty-five minutes. I'd have worked for free.

F. Lee Bailey came on the night he was announced as the defense counsel in the case of Albert DeSalvo, the so-called "Boston Strangler." DeSalvo, according to information, would have intercourse with his wife in the morning. Stop on the shoulder of the highway leading into the city, and masturbate. Then continue into town. Commit a rape. Then drive back from the city. Masturbate en route again. And then have relations with his wife that night.

F. Lee Bailey faced me. I asked him, "What was the first question you put to DeSalvo when you met?"

Bailey answered, "I wanted to know what his diet was!"

I've stuck my toe into the motion-picture-production water just twice. Each time I've been scalded, but one saga bears repeating.

I had read a book called *July, 1863*. It was by the late Irving Werstein. It told simply, but movingly, the story of the draft riots in New York in 1863, when the rich were able to buy their way out of "Lincoln's Nigger War" for $300, and the poor took their places. The blacks and the Irish were fighting each other for places on the lowest rung of the economic totem pole. The city, in the throes of a heat wave, was on the edge of a cataclysm. There were a weak mayor; an undermanned Union Army, most of it at Gettysburg; an equally undermanned police department; and angry mobs ranging the city, looting and burning as they went. They later lynched blacks in great numbers. I read the book and found that much of the area described in the book was still intact in New York and could be used in a film, with no need to build expensive sets.

I gave the book to Joseph E. Levine on a Friday. Someone must have read it to him over Saturday (I am told he never reads a book), and on Sunday I got a call from him asking for an option. I was thrilled! I optioned the book forthwith, and talked with Sidney Poitier about it, for there was a role of a black leader who, along with his neighbors, was given shelter from the mobs in the city jail, and armed by the police for self-protection. I talked with Eli Wallach, to play a brutal Union Army captain later stomped to death by the mob. To Diahann Carroll, to play the mistress of a bordello, whose lover (to be played by Paul Newman) was the leader of the uprising—a man who moved among the mob and talked of "niggers and black rule" while privately he was having a torrid affair with a "woman of color." She turned him in to the authorities, and he was put to death for bringing havoc to New York.

It had the makings of a great film, I thought. Months went by. Actors who had promised to cooperate were beginning to take other assignments. I asked Levine what was going on. He finally said, "The picture will cost four or five million—and besides, it'll cause trouble amongst the black groups." The project was dropped. Watts, and all the rest, followed. *Those* people didn't wait to see— or read—*July, 1863.*

If you tried to put the same cast together today, it would, for openers, be impossible. *If* you could afford it —you don't need the picture business.

So much for Levine's foresight. But, let's admit, he *did* make *The Graduate.*

Then there was my almost "movie actor" period. Eleanor Perry, foremost of the ladies who write, and eminently first as a screenwriter, was married to Frank Perry, who first came to fame, with her, when their film *David and Lisa* received critical acclaim and economic rewards. They did others. My favorite, *The Swimmer*, which starred Burt Lancaster, did not do well at the box office, but I thought it a powerful film. The Perrys, who had often been with me at the microphones, were a powerhouse combination—he as the director, she as the screenwriter. And success started to come their way.

The last time I saw Frank Perry, he was off to Spain to make a film called *Doc*. The screenplay this time was by columnist Pete Hamill, who wanted desperately to give up his almost daily chore of filing copy for the *New York Post* and devote himself to writing for films, and he had provided a fresh, different view of the Wild West hero Doc Holliday.

The film was being shot in the south of Spain—rugged country, which resembled the American Southwest, and much used by American filmmakers, who found crews, and budgets, much more to their liking there than in California or New York. Then too, foreign governments, anxious to attract movie people and the money they poured into the economy, made much more attractive deals for them than our own American society, which provides nothing by way of subsidy, tax shelters, and in many cases even police cooperation, to use a particular locale for the backdrop of a film.

For years, moviemakers sat, hat in hand, outside Mayor Robert Wagner's office, when he ran New York, and asked for city cooperation in the making of a film in the city. And there they sat. Then the television people took their place on the benches, for the cost of production in Manhattan and the moving of scenery from place to place was enormous. They wanted a central location, in mid-Manhattan, which could house, under one roof, everything they needed to provide live, dynamic programs. Wagner had no time to see them. So television moved to the West Coast. Motion pictures moved to foreign climes, from England to Tel Aviv. And finally Mayor Wagner moved from the Mayor's mansion to oblivion.

The new mayor, John V. Lindsay, couldn't bring television back to New York. The networks had already invested millions in real estate in the West, and hundreds of technicians, with their families, real estate purchases, school taxes, and supermarket buying power, had followed the studios to the West. With the breakup of the "big studios," and Mayor Wagner's political haze, most movie films were being made everywhere but in Hollywood and New York.

So Frank Perry was in Spain filming *Doc*. And Eleanor Perry was on the air with me, the night before she flew there, to see her husband and to check with professional eye on what had been filmed and how the movie was progressing. On the air she commented that I would be "perfect as a cowhand in the film." I ride, and I loved the idea of a trip to Spain, and a chance to write and comment on life in a "runaway movie" location. I would also enjoy the company of Frank Perry and Pete Hamill. I think Pete one of the best typewriter hands in the country. I told Eleanor I would be delighted. She promised to cable me the moment she arrived and tell me when to report.

I awaited word. I practiced wearing cowboy hats, and worked on my swagger. Nothing. I don't know what the word for it is in Spanish. But in English, what she found, I am told, when she arrived, was hanky-panky. She sued for divorce, and my movie career went out the window. Anyone want to buy a cowboy hat?

The French Connection was one movie that was shot

in New York. The director, William Friedkin, is a friend of mine. We first met at Hillard Elkins' apartment in New York. Hilly—the man who brought *Golden Boy* starring Sammy Davis, Jr., to Broadway, and then *Oh! Calcutta!*—was having a small bash. I was introduced to Friedkin, who was then a very young man, out of Chicago television, and had been making a film with Bert Lahr when Lahr died. That situation had required some great expertise from Friedkin in order to finish the film. Friedkin pumped my hand and made gracious comments about my broadcasts, such as "Man! I listen every night!" and "Yours is the best radio show in the country." Naturally, I warmed to him at once, detecting instantly his innate good taste and sensitivity.

He was then in preproduction for *The French Connection*. "Preproduction" means the months of planning a film—screenplay, locations, casting, financing, etcetera—before a movie actually goes before the cameras. I am always amused when I hear that a film has been "four years in the making." What they really mean is that it was in the lawyers' office for three years!

By now, *The French Connection* is history. It won Academy Awards. It made Bill Friedkin the "hottest" director in the industry, and when he followed up by directing the largest-grossing film in moviedom's history, *The Exorcist*, he became a millionaire. But at the time we met, his credits were minimal.

A bright, loquacious, and informed guy. I invited him to join me on the air. He came often, and he always had something important to contribute.

It is not generally known that the moneymen putting together *The French Connection* had to be sold on using Friedkin by the producer, Phil D'Antoni. They wanted a director with more impressive credits. D'Antoni fought for Bill, and won.

Afterward came Academy Awards night—which is really afternoon in Beverly Hills, because the television show is aimed for Eastern audiences and has to take into consideration the three-hour time difference. Friedkin's agent picked him up in a luxury car. Bill, who is indifferent to clothing, had rented a tuxedo for the occasion. There were about six passengers in the extravagant limousine. About two miles from the scene of the awards, the car broke down. They all coasted into a gas station. Nothing could resuscitate the car.

Bill spotted a young guy in a sporty jalopy at the gas pump. He approached him and asked if he'd like to make $20. The driver nodded his head, and Bill explained what had happened and that in a matter of minutes they were due at the awards ceremony. When the motorist found out that Friedkin had directed *The French Connection*, which he, the driver, had seen three times, he said, "Let me call my wife and tell her I'll be late—and then I'll take you!" Then, pausing, the driver said, "She'll think I'm drunk!"

A few minutes later, the driver pulled up at the awards site and discharged his formally dressed passenger cargo. In the lobby of the theater, the announcer was busily identifying the passengers being discharged from Rolls-Royces, Cadillacs, Bentleys, and Maseratis. He paid no attention to the battered crate that had dropped Friedkin, his agent, and their friends at the theater's entrance. The announcer looked at them as an English butler views those who should have come to the back door. An hour or so later, Friedkin was onstage accepting the industry's highest award for his direction of *The French Connection*. In his rented tuxedo!

A short time ago, at the height of the *Exorcist* storm, I asked him if he'd bought a tuxedo. He replied, "Yeah, I bought the one I rented! It fits fine!"

For all I know, A. E. Hotchner is wearing rented clothing too. Hotchner is the author of the best-selling book *Papa Hemingway*. He has also written countless articles for top slick magazines, and a great book about his boyhood in St. Louis. Hotchner, or "Hotch," as his friends address him, was walking his dog one night on Manhattan's fashionable East Side. He had just returned from Paris, where he had been on a buying spree at Cardin and other fashionable establishments that cater to the gentry. He was spending his *Hemingway* royalties royally, and was resplendent from cuff links to blazer.

When he returned from dog-walking, there was a beautifully dressed stranger on the other side of the door of his apartment house. The stranger held the door for him, and as Hotchner passed him, he said, "Thank you," and thought, What a good-looking outfit! When he entered his flat, he found closet doors open, drawers ransacked, and tie rack depleted. The stranger in the doorway had been dressed in Hotchner's newly purchased Paris wardrobe! And "Hotch" thought ruefully, No wonder I liked his tie—I picked it out!

One of the most frequent questions I get over the years is "How far do you plan your programs in advance?" The answer simply is—we don't!

You cannot think out a live program more than a day in advance, or sometimes that very day, particularly when news is breaking fast. Going back over my decades of programming, there are so many, many examples of a quick cancellation of what was planned and then what was actually on the air. From Golda Meir to Watergate, from *The Exorcist* to unexpected show-biz-personality confrontations, it's the "now" quality of the program that is, I feel, its most important ingredient. And the listeners, spoiled by that format though they be, have come to expect that at 10 each night, whatever has happened internationally, nationally, or locally that day will be discussed that night, and hopefully (if we can find them) by experts. This has had its funny, tragic, and moving overtones.

One night, Martin Baum, then an agent, dropped in with an old friend, film producer Martin Rackin. I was talking with Pauline Kael about her views on the films currently available that looked important enough to contend for Film Critics', Directors Guild, and Academy awards. She didn't like any of them, and proceeded to list some "winners"—all European-made, by European directors, and with European casts almost totally unknown to British or American audiences. A few weeks earlier she'd had a knock-'em-down two-hour battle with Artie Shaw, musician, author, and moviemaker, about American films, and she had then rapped them all. Artie had aptly pointed out that a filmmaker had to bring his product in with a profit or he'd never get an opportunity to make a second film. Miss Kael ignored his statements and spoke of "culture," and the hell with the profit motive.

Meanwhile, her grown daughter had sat on that occasion in the studio corner and thrust her index finger at me. I've never figured that out, for between Kael and Shaw I barely said a word, except "Please—one at a time," for they were all over each other.

Now Pauline was back, but alone, and having a marvelous time, for she was taking the opportunity to talk about the "smash" films of Transylvania and Timbuctoo.

When Rackin and Baum entered the studio, merely to watch and listen, I invited them to join us. When I introduced Rackin, I gave his credits on the air. Pauline Kael promptly attacked him for sullying the screen with "such trash." Rackin, a street-smart former New Yorker, looked across the table and said, "Why, you ugly, ignorant old broad—what the hell do you know about film?" Then he proceeded to lash her verbally. It may not have been very gentlemanly, but the score that night was Hollywood 90–Transylvania 0.

Then there was the night that the late Bobby Darin, a marvelous performer, and an Academy Award contender for his role in *Captain Newman, M.D.*, came to the microphones to tell of the success of his first open-heart operation. It was to be just one of his many visits. I thought his performance in *Newman* outstanding, having seen it in a screening weeks before its general release, and told Bobby on the air, when he appeared again, that he was sure to be nominated for an award. He didn't believe it. He was. He should have won. But he didn't, and then he lost the most important battle of all when he underwent surgery again. I grieved then, and I grieve now. For he was a remarkable young man, with a tremendous appeal onstage and off, and he made exciting "copy" whenever we met, always saying it "like it was."

There was the night that Judy Garland died, and thousands of New Yorkers jammed the streets around the funeral home waiting to say goodbye to one of the most unique and electrifying entertainers of our lifetime. The funeral over, we planned a tribute to Judy on the air.

It started with a very brief statement, and then, with a short pause each half hour for station identification, it rolled for two hours. It was winding up with *Judy at the Palace*, in which she'd pulled out all stops. I sat in the studio entrance, listening to the power of that performance and remembering the night it had been recorded.

At the time of the broadcast, Liza Minnelli; her then husband, Peter Allen; Kay Thompson, her godmother; and another friend were sitting quietly after the funeral in the Allens' apartment on East 57th Street in Manhattan. Someone suggested they get out of the apartment, break the dark mood, and take a ride. They left the apartment, got into the car, and pulled into the street. The driver punched on the car radio, and immediately the dial, set at WMCA, flooded the car with Judy's voice. It was eerie, I am told. There was Judy, on the radio, giving her heart to the audience at the Palace, while in fact, the world, and her close friends and family, had said goodbye to her for the last time earlier that day.

The driver quickly leaned over to change stations—but Liza said, "No, leave it." And they drove aimlessly around New York, and heard the entire program. They drank it all in, no one saying a word. And then Judy went into her finale of "Over the Rainbow," and from the back seat Liza was heard to say, "Go get 'em, Mama!"

But there were light moments, and there constantly are. Robert Taylor came to the studio. He was an even more attractive man in person than on any screen. He fully expected to talk film, and be asked inane questions like "Which leading lady do you prefer?" But his real love was animals, and the raising of them for fun and profit. I asked him about his ranch. His chickens. How he had gotten into it. How you breed chickens. How do you candle eggs? How do you get them to market? We went on like that for an hour.

He thought, at first, that I was putting him on. But then he warmed to the subject he loved. His farm, his animals, the outdoors. We chatted for an hour, and as he said good night, he laughed and said, "Goddamnedest interview I've ever had!"

Dr. Christiaan Barnard came to New York after his initial heart-transplant operations had made his name internationally known. A fascinating man and a loquacious guest, he told us in language I could understand how the operation was performed. We went on to theorize about the future. I asked what would happen if a 20-year-old youth's prostate gland were transplanted into a 70-year-old man's body. He thought for a moment and said, "It would probably shake the old man's chassis to death!"

Burt Lancaster came by. He hates to be interviewed, having been burned by interviewers who persisted in getting into his very private life. He guards his privacy and feels he is giving the interview merely to plug a picture, or something else that he's involved in. He was then immersed in a political fight in California about a proposed amendment on the ballot. He also knew that I had loved, publicly, a film called *Sweet Smell of Success*.

It was the Walter Winchell story. Winchell hated it, and never lost an opportunity, in his column or on the air, to blast it. Easy to understand why. For there on the screen, for the world to see, was his modus operandi. The bowing, scraping menials. The arm-twisting, through his column. The ass-kissing "public relations" men who fawned over him, since he was their bread and butter. His power was such that flacks (press agents) would charge a restaurant owner, or club owner, upwards of $100 per week, "guaranteeing" a frequent plug or mention in the Winchell column. They would then write a quip or crack about a celebrated person, and tack on the words, "when seen at ———," naming the watering hole. Winchell knew about their racket and encouraged it, for along with the plugs he fed like crumbs to diseased pigeons, he also had an army of flacks who were his eyes and ears, seeking out dirt and funneling it to him in the Cub Room at the Stork Club, run by his old buddy and a former bootlegger, the unctuous promoter Sherman Billingsley.

Most columnists of that day, and Earl Wilson still does it, did their own legwork—made the rounds nightly, asking maître d's, bandleaders, hatcheck girls who was there and what was news. Winchell put his bottom on a Stork Club banquette and moved only to his car to follow police calls, or to go to his barber, or to his apartment in a Manhattan hotel.

Burt Lancaster had captured the Winchell style perfectly. And Winchell didn't like what the truth of Lancaster's performance said to millions of moviegoing Americans. Nor have there been many better portrayals than the one that Tony Curtis delivered. The man he played as Winchell's pratt-boy I knew in real life. Curtis had done his movie homework well. I'm sure that many moviegoers saw the film and thought that a worm like the Curtis character didn't exist. He did, and so did Winchell—not the Broadway Beat Boulevardier he fancied himself, but the Winchell so aptly captured by Burt Lancaster in *Sweet Smell*.

The prime example of last-moment programming, and canceling of the originally scheduled appearances, occurred during the furor over the publication of the "Pentagon Papers." We had planned to do a show that night on the operations of the OSS during World War II. We had three former OSS agents booked for the show. Two hours before the program was to air live, a call was received from Sidney Zion, who had once been a reporter for *The New York Times* covering the law courts in New York; he is also an attorney, and had been

Assistant U.S. Attorney in New Jersey. He told me on the phone that he had a *big* news break for me, and would I clear the air for him to tell his story?

Zion had been a source of much volatile material for me in the past, and had never let me down. I trusted him, and said, "Okay." He said, "I'll be right over." I asked, "How long will you be?" He replied, "About twenty-five-minutes"—and then added, "My story is about the Pentagon Papers, and I will give the name of the man who took them on the air!"

I was excited, to say the least. I asked his permission to notify the network newsmen, the wire services, and *The Times* of his intentions. It was *The Times* which had first published the Pentagon documents, without revealing its source. Zion paused for a moment, and then said, "Sure, why not?" I hung up, and immediately called them all.

By the time Zion arrived at WMCA, *The New York Times* had one of its top reporters there (Murray Schumach), the *Daily News* had a reporter and photographer, and the wire services, the *New York Post*, and the networks had each sent a representative. Schumach tried to corner Zion as he got off the elevator. I stepped in and said, "Listen, I called you to allow you to hear Zion firsthand, but don't try to scoop me on my story!" He backed off. But a moment or two later the phone rang, and the call was for Zion from a member of the top brass at *The Times*. Zion took the phone and was asked by the editor-caller for the name of the purloiner of the papers. Zion replied, "If I give you the name of the man, will you tell me if I'm right?" He was told no. Zion laughed and said, "Then screw you—listen to the program like everyone else!"

Zion went on the air. He first explained why he had

come to me, rather than going to a network news program or seeking an appearance with Johnny Carson, Dick Cavett, or any of the other, larger avenues of exposure a story of his magnitude would rate. He said, "I know, Barry, that Peter Straus, who owns WMCA, does not dictate to you on your choice of guests, that he gives you free and untrammeled reign on who appears here, and those other places would put me through an interrogation of three lawyers before I got on the air." He also explained that the reason he was breaking the story that night was that the *St. Louis Post-Dispatch* had the same information, and the FBI, and they would break the story within a day. I asked, "Why don't you wait for the *Dispatch* story to break?" He replied, "Barry, I'm a reporter, and to me being first with the news is the name of my game. I don't want to be scooped by the FBI, the *Dispatch*, or anyone else."

Zion then named Daniel Ellsberg as the "culprit" in the Pentagon Papers swipe. The *New York Times* man, in the control room, had a telephone line open to his desk crosstown and kept whispering into the phone, and the listener at *The Times* could hear the control-room speaker booming out Zion's revelation. After Zion had made his remarkable statement, and scored a beat on the press and electronic news media of America, I invited the *Daily News* team to conduct an interview with him on the air. They got little more than a rehash of his original comments, and they left.

The *Daily News* the next day front-paged the story, with pictures. So did the *New York Post*. It was the lead item on the wire services, and in the *Los Angeles Times* and newspapers abroad. Of course, the *Daily News* left out the station call letters, and later apologized, saying it had made an "oversight" (Hmmmph!). But

The New York Times, that arbiter of "all the news that's fit to print," sat on the story for days, and finally broke it on an inside page, with no mention of where it had come from, or the drama surrounding it.

Zion, oddly, was blackballed by his colleagues, and Pete Hamill, in the *Post*, chastised him severely. Adam Walinsky, a Robert Kennedy aide when Bob was alive, and later candidate for Attorney General in the State of New York, called Zion at WMCA, after his revelation of the Ellsberg name, and furiously attacked him. The attack went out on the air, for the phone call was broadcast. He subsequently agreed to meet Zion two nights later and debate the issue with him, when by now the whole country indeed knew that it was Ellsberg, for the media revelations had been followed by action on the part of the FBI. Walinsky didn't budge, insulted Zion on the air left and right, and upon leaving, off the air, walked around him, toward the door, as though Zion had something catching. He then turned and said to Zion, "I think you're an unmitigated shit!"

Well, Hamill apologized to Zion, Ellsberg's case (at this writing) has been dropped, and the burglary of Ellsberg's doctor's office is no longer news, but Zion is still suffering blacklisting in many quarters for the crime of being a good newsman. I don't understand the ethic of his Coventry. It seems to me that those who had the story and *didn't* break it should be drummed out of the press corps. The day the media cease their adversary role, we will have a monarchy—and we damn near did!

But sometimes, when a guest's scheduling has to be set up from some distant place, an appearance is booked far in advance. Lana Turner was coming to New York. Her press people called and asked for air time for the star. You know it! I'd love to see what had gotten her that contract at Schwab's drugstore (an apocryphal story) years before! I plugged her upcoming appearance for three nights. The night of the broadcast, she simply didn't show up! No explanation, no call, no nothing. I chatted with the audience for a couple of hours, read some things of interest to me, and took a couple of calls.

The next day the phone rang. A sweet voice cooed, "Barry? This is Lana Turner. I want to apologize for last night. I wasn't feeling well, and must've fallen asleep and slept right through the night." It was a lie, I felt, but after all, how many times does Lana Turner call you? I thanked her for her explanation, and she promised to appear on the program a week later, when she returned to New York. I told that story to the audience that night, and announced that she would be on the following week, noting the night.

The night of her second scheduled appearance, a harried studio press agent appeared. He had been to her hotel suite to pick her up and accompany her to the studio. She was walking about, furiously beating her feet on the carpet, and she damned well wasn't going to make it once again. She said so in unprintable terms, and this time with no explanation. Can you figure that one out?

In the Pete Hamill screenplay *Doc*, as the central character, Doc Holliday, falters toward death, he soliloquizes that all he wanted to do in life was leave a "footprint." It is a line that sticks in the craw of every middle-aged throat, for you begin to question your being as you round the turn and head for the backstretch. Why am I here? What have I done? Where am I going? And finally, what's it all about? I have none of those answers yet, but I do have one small monument, which must be noted here. It's a tiny one, but it's mine. And it has stood the test of time.

It went into the planning stage when I first came to New York, out of the Army, and joined the announcing staff of WOR, in those days the flagship station of the Mutual Broadcasting System. From its studios at 1440 Broadway, at 40th Street (just below Times Square), its most famous programs originated, among them that of the late and highly regarded commentator Gabriel Heatter.

Heatter, who did a quarter-hour broadcast each night, was heard over 400 stations nationally, and his booming voice, and constant optimism when he reported "there's good news tonight," made him at one and the same time the most listened-to talker of his time and the most imitated, professionally and by mimics, on stages everywhere. He somehow managed to make "good news" out of Allied retreats, defeats, and losses, and always, editorially, pulled American chestnuts out of the World War II fire when things seemed their blackest.

I was assigned to Heatter. That sounds a hell of a lot more important than it was. All I had to do was wait until he had spoken for almost fourteen and a half minutes and then, at the microphone, say, "This program has come to you from New York. This is the Mutual Broadcasting System!" It was my proudest moment!

First off, it was just the chance to follow the great man; but more penuriously, it saved a lot of phone calls to the family in Los Angeles, and lots of postcards, pronouncing my good health and well-being. My mother listened to Heatter nightly, and when she heard her son utter that impressive sign-off, she knew all was well. Of course, within her circle I was immediately proclaimed "Gabriel Heatter's announcer"!

While Heatter was on the air, I generally sat in the corner of his small studio on the twenty-fourth floor of the building and listened to him; then, at the appropriate moment, I took the chair across the desk from his and signed the program off the air. At his left elbow there was a small, protruding black button. It was called a "cough button," and when pressed lightly it would turn off the microphone, allowing Heatter to clear his throat, and then, when he released the button, it would pop up into place at once and put him back on the air.

Heatter was broadcasting and going great guns one particular night. The Allied forces were on the move. The enemy was in disarray. Our economy was booming. And so was the Heatter voice. I became totally involved with what he was saying, and took my copy book, which all announcers carried, containing the daily log, assignments, and reports of performance, and put it on his desk as I sat in my chair and took in his every word.

Heatter looked up, past my shoulder—for I had my back to the control room—and saw pandemonium behind the glass. Engineers were scanning equipment; management men were flying into the control room. Heatter got a puzzled look on his face, but continued to speak. He looked quickly at me and pointed over my shoulder toward the control room. I turned and saw the turmoil going on in there, and couldn't imagine what all the excitement was about.

Suddenly, from behind the glass, all eyes focused on me and then down at my book. It was lying flat across Heatter's cough button, and had taken him off the air for the interminable seconds it had been lying there. The studio door flew open, in the midst of his broadcast. I was grabbed by my shoulder; my book was snatched from the desk, releasing the button; and both of us were flung from the studio. Heatter had been off the national network for almost a minute!

The incident led to voluminous reports to stations

across the country, I was damn near fired, and the next day a small, circular aluminum collar was placed around every cough button in the WOR studios, installed so that the collar stood half an inch above the button to protect it. Ever after, in order to depress it, one had to insert a finger into the circle of aluminum, clear one's throat, then lift the finger in order to go back on the air. Those protective devices, I am told, are still there. That is my footprint. No one else can make that statement. And Gabriel Heatter, to his death—and to his credit—laughed whenever he told the story.

The nicest assignment ever was the chance to go to Rome, Italy, to interview motion-picture director John Huston for *Playboy* magazine. He was directing George C. Scott and Ava Gardner in *The Bible*, an ambitious undertaking being made in one of the huge studios outside Rome built by Dino De Laurentiis. Huston used monumental new photographic equipment in his endeavor to put the story of the Good Book on film. Next door, on another stage, Charlton Heston was making *The Agony and the Ecstasy*, and each day I would see him in the paint-spattered attire of Michelangelo.

On the set of *The Bible*, George C. Scott would sit off camera, in a camp chair, wearing phenomenal makeup, for he was playing Abraham at the age of 80. And along with spirit gum, and man-made wrinkles, and a scraggly beard, he smoked his Camels and mumbled about the "shitty life of an actor getting up at four to put on makeup!" One scene called for Ava Gardner, lying on a pallet in front of the camera, to hold up a newly born male child and say, "Abraham—here is your firstborn."

They rehearsed the scene—repeatedly. They used a doll for the baby's stand-in, and then when everything seemed right they would bring the baby onto the set, with its mother; the mother would relinquish the child to Ava, after removing the many layers of clothing the newborn was wearing; and now, with the naked baby, the scene would begin. This after much yelling, in Italian, to members of the crew to be "silent!" "Stop eating!" "Stop playing cards!" And once more, "*Silenzio!*"

Scott would wearily get up from his chair, walk onto the set, kneel beside Gardner, and get a few brief, softly spoken directions from Huston, who would then walk to his chair placed beneath the mammoth camera and say quietly, "That looks fine; let's take it." As the camera would start to roll, the baby, held first at Ava's breast and then raised aloft to be handed to Scott, would in his nakedness feel the chill of the studio after the warmth of his swaddling clothes, and he would urinate. He urinated first on Scott's nose. The next time on his ear. The next time on his cheek. Once on his head. This went on for *six days!* And finally Scott blew up. He yelled, "I didn't come to Rome to get pissed on!"

I found Huston the gentlest of men. We conducted our interview, talking into a tape machine between set-ups, in rest periods, and at lunch hour. We had talked before in New York (and have talked since), but he had become an Irish national, and I asked him why. Originally he fudged the question—perhaps he was taking my measure; so we switched to his life-style, horses, and drinking companions, and then on the last day together, as we crossed each other's paths outside the studio, he handed me a piece of paper. I still have it. It says:

You asked me earlier why I chose to live in Ireland. Ireland is the nearest thing I imagine to what the world was like in the United States before the Civil War. It's an antebellum life. It's nothing to drive three or four hours for dinner, or to spend time at someone else's home, days at a time. You don't stay in a hotel in Ireland unless you go to Dublin, perhaps—people stay in your house, you stay in their house. It may be the most bigoted country, yet at the same time, it's the most tolerant. There's no such thing as an eccentric in Ireland—everybody's eccentric. It's a great place to bring up children. Sometimes I doubt that it *is* a great place for that because it doesn't prepare them for the life that's bound to come. So it's one of two things you have to decide for your children; you either prepare them by living elsewhere, or you live in Ireland and give them a marvelous childhood to fall back on while they're licking their wounds later on in life!

Scrawled in Huston's hand on an additional page is written, *Nothing disgusts me—unless it's unkind or violent.*

It is one of the few interviews I've kept after more than 40,000. I treasure this one for its kindness, gentility, and humanity. The others I've saved? The Al Jolson interview, and the Robert Kennedy interview the last time he came to the WMCA studio. I played it after his death. It was an eerie forecasting of his death, as though he knew his end would be violent. For I asked him of his future. He thought, and replied, "I never plan tomorrow—I've learned not to do that, considering the events of my past life."

It's only accident that I have those; the others were simply erased. And I mean simply—for it was pure simplemindedness. If those interviews over the years had been saved, they could serve as a completely unique library on contemporary history of the day. But tape gets erased as a matter of course, and economics sees that it does even sometimes when you mark DON'T ERASE on it.

I did that after a marvelous assignment in Rome. It was 1963—the year of the Papal inauguration, and the year of the JFK visit. For six weeks I covered the Rome scene. Each morning at 9 we would tape two hours of talk with celebrated tourists passing through, members of the Vatican, motion-picture people in town, newsmen, and so forth.

The program taping ended at 11 A.M. Five minutes later a little truck from Alitalia Airlines came by the Radio Italia studios and a hand came out the driver's window. The tape—wrapped, sealed, and addressed—disappeared into the truck, was rushed to the airport, and was given to the pilot of the flight bound for New York at 1:20 P.M., Rome time. It was flagged for U.S. Customs, which had cleared it in advance of our Rome assignment, so that it went right through and was then delivered to WMCA by special messenger. The flight arrived in New York at 5:30 P.M. That very night it was on the air in New York. Alitalia didn't miss a broadcast in six weeks—even once when the flight had to lay over an hour in Boston.

Once there was live coverage from the Vatican itself, when the Papal inauguration took place. I was assigned the vantage point of the Bernini columns. That is, the broadcast booth on *top* of the columns which embrace the entrance to Vatican City. From there I looked down on a pageant that was unbelievable in its ritual, color, ceremony, and magnificence. It was late afternoon when His Holiness began his address to the assembled thousands in the square, while millions listened and watched the world over. As the late-afternoon sun constantly changed its pattern of light, and with the crowds moving, the pattern of sound changed and a picture was created never to be forgotten. That night, Romans and Italians in the millions watched the skies as fireworks announced the beginning of a reign.

I still have that press pass. But no tapes. The station erased them!

And now to the finale, and the most difficult part to write. It has to do with marriage.

How does it begin?

Or more to the point—how does it end?

You say to yourself, It began because you were in love. And there were two marvelous children. A son and a daughter, now both grown. Both married, and parents themselves. The son a graduate of a military academy, and making his career in space work in NASA. The daughter happily married and a mother, after a long, successful career, climbing steadily upward with a large fashion magazine to an editorship.

So what happened to your own marriage? You started with nothing. Fourteen dollars in your pocket the night you were married. No honeymoon, for you had to work. But things got a lot better in Miami Beach. They became fantastic when you returned to New York. You were meeting marvelous people, out every night, loving your work, making more money than you believed possible.

But what happened?

Beth was a beautiful girl. She is a handsome woman. Great mother. Fine homemaker. But chinks began to appear in the seemingly solid armor of the marriage a long time ago. Minor bickering at first. Full-fledged arguments at last. Private at first. Then loud enough to be heard through the walls of a large apartment. Then the battleground moved to public places. The street, the restaurant. Mutual friends gradually started to withdraw.

Granted, many of them moved West, but we called them. Why didn't they call back? Or is it no fun to be with people who find no fun being with each other?

Our tastes became noticeably different. In books. In people. In movies. In general. I felt enormous guilt. I felt less and less like staying home when I had the studio to go to. I started to go there earlier and earlier. I dreaded the weekends, for it meant staying in to bicker, or going out to fight. An evening that started pleasantly enough ended with grimness over things that one could not put one's finger on or explain rationally.

I thought of analysis. I needed help. I couldn't believe what was happening to us, the "perfect couple." One night, at the height of a furious row, the phone rang. It was Sidney Poitier. Poitier? My God! He might be my lifesaver! He called at the very moment when I needed him! For I had seen Sidney on Madison Avenue once, long before, as he came out an office building, and he had said, "Oh, I was coming from my analyst. She's marvelous—she's turned my whole life around. My career, my thinking—she's fantastic!"

I told Sidney that I was emotionally drained. That I desperately needed professional guidance. Would he ask his analyst if I could see her once, and perhaps she could recommend someone I could talk to professionally? He listened, I thought attentively, and he then said, "Let me get right back to you."

I have never heard from Sidney Poitier since!

It got worse. I was now going directly from fury at home to "Good evening, ladies and gentlemen" on the air—and conducting interviews with my mind as fragmented as a basket of jigsaw pieces. I sometimes felt that I couldn't continue the program.

I respected Beth. I admired her. I felt compassion. I

felt enormous guilt. For somehow I had wronged her. I sought my own analyst, and I consulted him for a year. He died. And then another, who became my life raft. He was used to people with crazy hours, and allowed me to call him at any time, and over weekends and holidays.

He heard me out, often, and the theme would repeat itself. He said, "You can give her everything but you. That you cannot do. Save yourself and her. Life is just once around." I thought of that much later when I read Garson Kanin's great book *A Thousand Summers*—where it is written, "Everyone dies, the trick is to live before you do—and not so many do that."

I had also conned myself into believing that no one noticed the terrible strain we were both under. I was wrong. Everyone noticed. And a great many people discussed it. During that period I hurt my back. As I lay in bed, nursing myself and being nursed by her, a period of calm prevailed. And finally we talked—openly, for the first time—about separation. When I was better, I moved to a hotel.

I moved back.

I moved out again.

And moved back again.

I moved back seven times.

I moved out eight.

We were legally separated in 1971.

We were divorced in 1973.

And the tomorrows began.

BARRY GRAY WITH ED SULLIVAN

GRAY: The man that I'm about to introduce speaks very well himself. Here is Ed Sullivan of the New York *Daily News*. Ed, I know that you have many things to say and I'd just like to ask you to take over and later I may ask a couple of questions.

SULLIVAN: Fine. Well, first of all, Barry, I'd like to say you must have the most amazing audience in all of the field of communications, because I never received so much mail, I've never received so many phone calls, and surprisingly enough, as I noted in my own correspondence in answering the letters, when you embark on a controversial subject, you're always going to get two answers to it: one for and one against. And this thing surprised me because it was so heavily for. I'd say the ratio is about ninety-eight percent to two percent. And that's the thing that astounded me. . . . I think that a lot of accolades are due you for supplying to the city of New York, which should have it, an open forum where two sides of the case can be presented. And where you never pull any punches in inviting both sides of the case, just as you did in the case that I came in on, that I wasn't called in on, on which I had volunteered to come in on. Now, in the two percent of the letters that came in, in the two percent of letters questioning, I've been asked in these letters and postcards, why did I come on this program to get into the—what loosely can be described as—the "Winchell–Josephine Baker Case." Well, that's a very fair question. And if you step up on a stand and you pop off, then the people who listen in are entitled to ask that ques-

176

tion whether it's two percent or one percent or one-tenth percent. But actually, the people who ask that question are not very familiar with my record, because although it was my first appearance on this microphone, actually I've been here a long, long time ago. A long time ago. Long before Barry Gray was here and long before Chandler's was here, and long before some of you youngsters in the room were here. Because twenty-four years ago, I was then a sporting editor, and New York University booked a game against the University of Georgia to be held in New York, and I got the contract for the game—which was not very difficult because they generally were accessible to the sporting editors— and the contract of the game said that N.Y.U. had played Georgia University in New York and the stipulation was made, to which New York University agreed, sub rosa, that the Negro star of the N.Y.U. team would be benched for four quarters. And I wrote then—that's twenty-four years ago—that if intercollegiate athletics had sunk to that low a level where the gate receipts were the thing, where it was more important to make money on a big game in New York than it was to humiliate one man, whether he was an Irish Catholic or a Jew or a Protestant or a Negro, then I suggest that N.Y.U. cancel the game and give up football. So I go back a long, long way in this field. A long way. And the reason I came here was not because of any personal animosity toward Winchell. I despise Walter Winchell because he symbolizes to me evil and treacherous things in the American setup. That's why I came here, and I came here knowing that it was an open forum. And I said that I would very happily be on this same stand with Walter Winchell and tell him to his face that I despise him and explain why I despise him knowing full well that he could then turn to me and answer me. So this wasn't any one-way deal. I came in here as an American because I felt this issue and all the allied issues were important enough to be threshed out publicly and to illustrate where evil was quartered and where goodness was quartered. I say I've been here a long time ago.

I've been writing in New York for thirty-one years. Long before the infant state of Israel was recognized as a state. In my column I suggested that the Jew in Israel and in the United States and all over the world read the pages of Irish history. That the only way they were going to win their statehood was by the shedding of blood, just as the Irish did. And I certainly don't feel any more a stranger sitting here than Parnell or Robert Emmett, both Irish Protestants, must have felt when they led the Irish Catholic revolt in the south for Irish freedom. I go back a long way in the Israeli history. When Israel needed a food train some years ago, I had the privilege of acting as chairman of the national effort to get it. In the forests of Israel there's a tree planted in the name of the Sullivans for the work I've been privileged to do in the Israeli cause at Madison Square Garden in another national effort. In the case of the Italians—my dear little paisanos—when the movies embarked on a campaign of naming all villains in moving pictures Italians, I came out and did a column on it and said this was evil. When Archbishop Stepenac and Cardinal Mindszenty were imprisoned by the Communists, I did column after column calling attention to the evil of this. Some years back, Bill Robinson put on a big benefit show in Miami, and Miami never had permitted an all-white show or a white-and-Negro show to raise funds for a Negro charity. And Bill Robinson called me up and said, "would you come over to the Miami ball park and participate in this show?" I said, "I'll be there at any hour you designate." And we put that show on. Now, I'm saying these things in all humility because I consider them all privileges to have participated in each one of them. But the question has been asked of me and I'm going to answer it to the very best of my ability. Now, years later it came to pass that Bill Robinson, tired and exhausted from playing thousands and thousands of benefits, and I say that literally, came to a point where his heart had given out and Bill Robinson was broke, which is no disgrace because we all have been broke, and we may all be broke before the final tax setup is accomplished.

But it seemed to me then that this was a magnificent opportunity to demonstrate to all of the Negro youngsters of Harlem that here was a great man. Bill Robinson had suffered because he had opposed the Paul Robesons and the radicals of his race and he had come out openly and attacked them, and I thought that this was a magnificent chance to prove to all of the Negro youngsters, not only of Harlem, but of the country, that even though he died broke, that the nobility which had attached itself to Robinson in his lifetime as a great show-stopper shouldn't be waived in death. And I had the great privilege then in pursuing that thought of organizing a group of public-spirited New Yorkers—and I explained this to 'em. I explained it to Bill O'Dwyer, and I said, "Bill, I know you're not feeling well, but on this day you must come uptown and you must deliver a funeral oration for Bill Robinson." And I got ahold of Milton Berle. And I got ahold of Mrs. Irving Berlin—Irving was out of town—and I got ahold of Ethel Merman, and I got ahold of the top stars of the white stage, and I said, On this day you must come up to this church in Harlem and I want you to act as the ushers. And then we got ahold of the Board of Education, and the Board of Education persuaded —not persuaded—the Board of Education agreed that this thing was so important in the fabric of our country that all children would be given time off—there'd be no school starting at noon. And that funeral started in Harlem with all of these great white stars there—Jimmy Durante was there, Danny Kaye, and I put one of each—we engaged thirty-six limousines and I said they must be the shiniest and finest-looking limousines that ever came through Times Square. Because Bill is going to go out as a champ, as he lived. As we came down through Harlem, I have never seen such a sight in all my life. From 138th Street all the way out to the cemetery in Brooklyn, the streets were lined with people. But the thing that struck me deepest and seemed most important to me that the streets of Harlem were lined from 138th Street down to 96th Street, when we turned into Central Park

179

West, and here are all of these little Negro youngsters and they pointed out these people in cars . . . they said, "There's Durante" . . . you could see them mouth the words. And there was no rushing for autographs—these kids understood what this meant. That the top people of the white stage were saluting and saying goodbye to one of the greats of the Negro stage. One of the greats of the American stage. These things have been done. And I've had a chance to do them. Joe Louis became the heavyweight champion of the world, I talked to Joe and I said, "Joe, from now on you're not just a Negro athlete; you're a symbol of a whole race." And I said, "You must live that way accordingly." He needed no urging. Joe Louis is one of the finest human beings I've ever met. With the greatest sense of proportion, the finest sense of dignity, the finest sense of decency. And Joe Louis loves to play golf, and I played golf with him up at his club one day. It was sort of a semiprivate club, the old Oak Ridge Club up near Mount Vernon. And I said to him, "Joe"—he just loves the game—I said, "Tomorrow let's play at my club." And he sort of laughed, and he said, "It might be better if we played at my club." And I say, "By no means." So I played with him at the Quaker Ridge Country Club. And I played with him and Bob Hope and Hal LeRoy out at Ridgewood in New Jersey. And later on there was a big Communist rally in Harlem and a Negro agitator, a Commie, got up and said, "If you think I lie to you when I say how you're imposed upon by the whites," he said, "your heavyweight champion of the world is sitting out there." He said, "He's a former GI, he loves to play golf." He says, "I challenge Joe Louis to tell me if he's permitted to play on a course with whites." And Louis came up out of the audience and he said, "Yes, I have been." He said, "Where did you play?" He said, "I played at the Westchester Country Club," he said, "I played at Quaker Ridge," and he said, "I played at Ridgewood." And the reaction was so violent that the agitator was chased right out of the park. Now, these are the way things happen accidentally, but they're all a pattern of life. And that's the pattern of life that I've tried to follow. I'm not the smartest person in the world, God knows, but I know in all humility that you can't hurt one part of the human body. You can take my hand here as this illustration. You can't chop off the tip of a finger of this hand without affecting the whole hand—the disease spreads, and in the human body, and the international body, and the racial body. You can't persecute a Jew at this tip of the finger without having the infection spread to the Irish Catholic, who then is persecuted. And once the bulldozers establish those beachheads, then they go on to persecute the Protestant, and then they start hating a man because he eats meat while he eats vegetables. It just can't be done. You can't be a rabble-rouser, you can't call for persecution, you can't slander one person or one race without it affecting every part of the racial body. And that's the way I've tried to live my life. I've tried to live it because that's the way I was taught by my mother and father. They weren't the smartest people in the world, but by God, they were decent. And in Port Chester there was no such thing as distinctions. I played on teams in Westchester County when I was at Port Chester High School against Negroes and Jews and Protestants and other Catholics and it made no nevermind. When Jackie Robinson first came into the big leagues and some of the great minds of baseball suggested it was perfectly all right to throw beanballs at him, I wrote columns in opposition to that. I thought that was evil. On our television show, I have believed that television, to pay its debt for the use of the public air, must use itself wisely and well as an instrument for the public good. And I have felt—and I know from my conversations with Southerners who are rabidly anti-Negro because they didn't know, not because of venom in them, they just didn't know—that when the Ink Spots, when they saw Billy Eckstein in their living rooms and when they saw the Pearl Baileys, that they got a completely different picture of the Negro. And I feel that television has been able to accomplish a tremendous job of goodwill, and there's nothing we need in this country and in the world as much as goodwill. So it's made no difference, and again I say this in all humility. If I've ever been called upon by the Jewish Federation to raise money—and I think I ran their first all-star show in New York, through the intervention and solicitation of a friend of mine, the late Anatol Friedland; I put on the first hundred-dollar-a-plate dinner for the Jewish Federation in New York—and if the Red Cross called on me and if little Catholic parishes have called on me and if Protestant groups have called on me—I don't care what they are; if the Nisei—I spend a lot of time writing about the Nisei, the wonderful work of the great Japanese Americans in World War II—and it's never made any difference to me who they were or if their faith was my faith, which is Roman Catholic. That made no nevermind. I've tried to live out the pattern of my life that way. I'm reminded, and I go along with Barry in feeling that you can't let the cycle go too far, that you can get to a point of hysteria in a country or in a group where hysteria will forfeit the very liberties you fight for. And I'm reminded of Alfred E. Smith. Some years back there were a group of Socialists elected to the New York Legislature and they were barred from their seats and Alfred E. Smith, who was a Catholic, he came out and headed a committee, which included Charles Evans Hughes and the greatest minds of the Bar Association in New York, and fought this thing and said this was evil. I've gone through all of these things because I've been asked why I came here. I came here in the ordinary day-by-day pattern of my life. I came here as an American. I thought a shameful thing had been done. A woman had made a protest of discrimination, and whether that protest was founded in extreme sensitivity or not, that made no difference. I know if Abraham Lincoln had been presented with the same sort of a problem he would have gotten in touch with a Josephine Baker and apologized to her and said that if what seemingly was rudeness had affected her, he would apologize to her for it. Now, there is great nobility of thinking. There is greatness of thought there. He had power, but he had great humility. But I despise anyone who uses power to blackjack people. If we speak up— Now, in Winchell's column, over and over again, in his most maudlin vaudeville moments, he repeats a phrase, and he's very fond of it. It sort of rolls around in his typewriter and it comes spraying out. It's a quotation from Voltaire, and I say Winchell has repeated this time and again in his column: "I disapprove of what you say, but I will defend to the death your right to say it." If I've read that once in Winchell's column, I've read it fifteen times. "I disapprove of what you say, but I will defend to the death your right to say it." Josephine Baker said something of which he disapproved. I ask you—did he defend to the death her right to say it? No, he didn't. In answering her, and the answer wasn't called from him, nobody asked him for the answer, but in his megalomania, he was so burned up that this one voice had risen to question any particle of property or any area of which he was a friend, he called her a Fascist, he called her a Communist, he called her anti-Semitic, and then capped it all by calling her anti-Negro. This was because, in the words of Voltaire, she had spoken up. She had expressed the right, the God-given right, to say something. But instead of defending it with his death, he proposed to convert it into her suicide as a performer and as a human being. And then Josephine Baker came to this microphone on two nights, and in a very carefully documented and in a very carefully dignified answer to these allegations, she submitted record that far from being with Vichy France, she indeed had won the French Medal of Resistance. That the French Government had acclaimed her one of the great heroines of World War Two. That she had risked her life, she had risked her professional reputation, obviously she had risked death as a spy to carry out very dangerous missions for the French underground and the allies. And in a very carefully documented case, she answered the allegation that she was anti-Negro by pointing out she lived at the Hotel Theresa in Harlem. That she had shopped in Harlem shops, that she had enjoyed and tried to get Negro patronage. This I know to be true personally, because I've been at the *Folies Bergère* in Paris—I never met Josephine Baker; to me she was just another performer on the other side of the footlights, albeit a real good one—but there were Negroes at the *Folies Bergère*. So I know that statement's wrong. She answered that statement that she was anti-Semitic by submitting the fact that her husband was Jewish. In short, she answered every charge made against her. Charges made recklessly and with great abandon. He, confident in his power and buoyed by the fact that no New York newspaper except one had taken this thing up, because they didn't want to give him publicity on it— I say that he's a megalomaniac and a dangerous one. In *Time* magazine this week, the issue of January seventh, *Time* asked him for a reply to the statements I had made about him. Winchell said, "I refuse to answer. I didn't hear what Sullivan said. I'm only interested in what the President of the United States says about me." Now, this is really a big man. This is a very, very big and important man. I mean, when any one of us gets to the point— If I were to say to you, standing here, "I don't want to talk to Barry Gray, or to you, I speak only to the President of the United States," you're going to call the men in the white jackets and take me away from here, unless my wife does it before you do. This man will speak only to the President of the United States. I ask you, what nobility of thinking, what dignity of utterance would prompt any imbecile to make any such a statement as that? We all pay taxes, we're all taxpayers, but we do have a reasonable suspicion that the President of the United States is a fairly busy man. He's got great affairs of state to attend to, in a most troubled world. This man will only pick up the phone if the President of the United States is announced as his caller. Now, I say I despise him as a newspaperman. I say he's traduced every ethic of the newspaper world. The first time I ever went to Hollywood to write a column out of there for the *News*, they said to me, "Do you want a private phone in your house?" I said, "I've never heard of a newspaperman having a private phone. We're supposed to get news and people are supposed to be accessible to give us news." I was amazed at this aristocracy of Hollywood writers who had private phones because I know my managing editor on the *News* would throw me right out on East 42nd Street if I proposed that I conduct my business that way. This man not only has a private phone, but he speaks only to the President on the private phone—if he's good enough to give the President the phone number. I talked about humility. Jimmy Durante is a pretty nice paisano. And one of the finest songs he ever sang was a song that wound up by saying, "All tombstones read alike." And that is very true. We pass through this vale of tears. If we catch lightning in a bottle, we pass through it in a fairly dignified fashion. We have enough to send our children to school, we have enough to ensure some dignity of life, for our families and our relatives, and then we come one day to a decent and reverent grave. But all tombstones do read alike. And I despise any human being who forgets it. Because when you forget humility, when humility ends, when you picture yourself as Winchell pictures himself— and I've known him for a long, long time—when you picture yourself as a little Hitler, able to tell the big lie over and over again and ruin somebody who speaks up against you, I tell you then that that man is in a dangerous state, and I tell you that a country which is exposed to his ravings and his rantings is in a more dangerous state. I said the other night on this microphone, this man didn't know the facts of Josephine Baker. He didn't know 'em because, first, his attack on her must have been inspired by venom. But he didn't know for a larger and broader reason. He didn't know France. Because this man who poses as an expert on the international setup, who dictates the disposition of the Marshall Plan, who tells you what Italy should do and what Ireland should do and what England should do and coins rather crude jokes about the Prime Minister of England and our other allies, never has been across the ocean; he's never been to any of these countries. And yet he sets himself up as an international expert. I doubt that he's ever been in an airplane. I've heard him speak with great authority on how many air groups we should have. I know that he personally attacked Jim Forrestal, who was a fine, decent American, a wonderful—and who died because he just couldn't stand persecution and everything that went with it. So I've answered all of these things. I've said all of these things at length, Barry, because some of them have asked me why I came here. I came here because I'm an American. I came here because for the last twenty-four years in New York I've gone wherever I could to fight whatever I could that manifested itself as inimical to our country. Now, a lot of people wrote in, and I was very amazed at it. They congratulated me on what they called or characterized as my bravery in attacking Walter Winchell. Well, actually, I wasn't attacking Winchell, not as a person. I was attacking him as a symbol of things that I feel to be evil. But bravery, bravery in talking back to him or talking back to anybody who's intent on hurting or destroying the American fabric, I think that's carrying it too far. I'd say that— I had a youngster on our show tonight, a Major Gerharra, a kid from Wichita, Kansas, shot down five Korean jet planes. Started out in Wichita High School and never went beyond that. Enlisted in the Army and then the Air Force. Learned enough about aviation and astronomy and navigation and has become a top American ace. When that kind of a man is on the stage with you, you're associating with bravery, and in our audience one night we had General Jonathan Wainwright of Corregidor. That, in that case, you're associating and standing close by and are reflected in the aura of great courage and bravery. Carlson, the Danish skipper out in the Atlantic, sticking to a ship that's almost turned turtle. That's bravery. I tell you very honestly that no such equivalent bravery, not even in the precincts of that type of bravery, were involved in this. When I sit at a microphone and say I despise Walter Winchell, I despise him because to me he has become dangerously anti-American. He has joined up with the legions of character assassins such as a Senator McCarthy. He represents everything to me that is most hateful in power, entrenched power. He lacks humility, the humility that was exemplified by an Abraham Lincoln, the humility that's exemplified by a Cardinal Spellman in leaving St. Patrick's Cathedral to go to Korea and celebrate Masses out there for the kids. These are great men. These are great Americans, they're great human beings. I don't think that Winchell is a great American anymore. I think that something has happened to him. I don't know what it is, but I think that the effects of it are evil. And this has been a great pleasure for me to come here as an American, and against the background of my own record in this city, and to tell you these things that I feel very strongly about him. And the last time I was here I said I would enjoy having him come to the microphone. And sitting here with him at the microphone and reasoning this thing out or threshing it out, because he's had the same opportunity that I've had. And the reason I came here, honestly, is this: When the Josephine Baker thing started on this mike and when Josephine Baker came here, I knew that performers and people in the profession would hesitate to come to Barry Gray—at least, I felt that. And I called up Barry Gray because I wanted to underscore and say as an American that what he had done was fine, and decent . . . and should be done, and that if he ever wanted me to fill in any spot on his program, if ever there was an occasion when he didn't have enough guests—he always has them—but that if ever the occasion arose that he didn't have 'em, to please call me up. That as an American, I would be very proud to

187

come here and help him out for a magnificent American job that he has done here at this microphone. Thank you very, very much.
(APPLAUSE)

GRAY: Thank you, Ed.
(APPLAUSE)

GRAY: Ladies and gentlemen, and Mr. Ed Sullivan, in days to come, there will be much conversation about what has happened here tonight and what went before. I hope and trust that the people of the city of New York and the people that will become acquainted with the facts of this story will long remember Mr. Ed Sullivan. The (APPLAUSE). If you don't mind, I'm going to just talk around a point. It may sound like double-talk for a second, but you think about it rather carefully. When Ed Sullivan first called me—and it's quite true, every word that he said, just exactly the way he said it—he called up originally, and said that he wanted to congratulate me upon an American job, and I said to him practically what he said here tonight about himself: there hasn't been any bravery shown at this microphone. It's purely and simply a question of an individual, one Josephine Baker, being attacked over and over and over again and not having a voice of her own. She was invited to partake of our "voice." Just as simple as that. You remember the Josephine Baker night, or two nights, that she was here. I said nothing. I merely read a couple of copies of things that she had presented to me, and I was proud of the opportunity to best exemplify what I think the radio and television business should do—give people an opportunity to express themselves, defend themselves, or work for issues that are important. Immediately after that discussion, Mr. Sullivan called me and said just exactly what he said here tonight. That if ever I needed a guest, or if ever I wanted anything because of this situation, because he said I would be attacked, kindly call. And I asked, "May I talk about this phone call?" And he said to me then a very important thing which I should like to highlight here. Let it be noted. This is a peculiar business we're in. Performers are wonderful people, and I'm sure they will understand that the love emanated from this microphone for them is an honest feeling. I understand because of that feeling for them the position that they're in. They don't feel, and I agree, that they can afford to risk the enmity of an important newspaperman. And Ed Sullivan knew this too. And I dug, as they say colloquially, the real reason that he called. Oh, he called, sure, to say a nice thing. And he called to offer his service, but the real reason he called was shown when he said, Yes, you may use my name, because he knew that the moment I announced that he called and said congratulations, that performers who might be worried about reprisals against them would now think, Well, there might be reprisals from one quarter, it's true. But there is an equally important friend, if not more important, in another quarter. That's what happened then. Now, I shan't say anything about discussions of reprisals aaginst this broadcast. Mr. Sullivan pointed out a week ago or ten days ago that I could expect to be smeared. I can. There is much activity going on behind the scenes on all fronts. And one day soon, I imagine, you will have an opportunity to hear all the stories, but I am firmly resolved that this shall not resolve itself into a personal fight between me and anybody else or anybody else and Ed Sullivan. Mr. Sullivan and I agree that this is purely an issue of character assassination and ask, Can an individual with power destroy the character of another? Mr. Sullivan and I believe that this is un-American. We feel that if reprisals are to come, then we must defend ourselves. We are prepared to defend any attacks that come. But let the attacks come first from the other quarter. Never let it be said that this was an offensive battle. And I pointed out to Mr. Sullivan, the other night on the phone, another reason why I'm glad he's here. If I had started this and said the things that Ed said here tonight, I would have been accused by people of looking for something bad. In a nice thought, they would have said, Well he's a young fella trying to get attention by attacking a national figure. That would have been untrue. Completely untrue. But you can't defend yourself against an attack of that kind, an insidious thing that finds itself around the street known as Broadway. When Ed Sullivan came here they couldn't say it because he is already famous in an international sense. He is already wealthy in any sense. There is no reason—financial or professional—for Ed Sullivan being here tonight except that he is an American and a great one. But I want to point out to you, in case you hadn't thought of it, that there is absolutely no personal gain that he could make by his appearance at this microphone. And no one can accuse him of this behind the appearance. Ladies and gentlemen. This promises to be a very dirty, very underhanded fight. Many pressures will be brought to bear. Much mud will be thrown at all parties concerned on this side. But I want you to remember what was said here tonight and now. That never once was any mud originated from this microphone from any of the guests or by myself. It all came as a defense. A defense for a woman that had only complained about rudeness in a nightclub—only rudeness—and for this she was called Communist, Fascist, anti-Negro, anti-Semitic, anti-American. She has been insulted; there was an attempt to destroy her professional career. This is what is meant by character assassination. Mr. Sullivan made an important point when he said that you cannot cut off a hand without harming the body. This is a great and wonderful thought that goes down in history. People that feel as Ed Sullivan have been fighting this kind of fight for years. It's the people that fight this kind of fight that made progress. And to a most progressive gentleman, and I use the word "gentleman" advisedly, and to a most progressive audience, and to a fine group of American people who have sent the letters that have given us the courage and the determination to stick this through, I say thank you, and I wish again to gain, if you will, another accolade for a wonderful man, Ed Sullivan. (APPLAUSE) I want to add some names to a roll of honor that we are starting. A roll of honor of people with guts. Ben Blue is in the audience. Thelma Carpenter is in the audience, Nat Brandywine is in the audience, Michelle Farmer is in the audience, Marlo Lewis, Toby Arden, Jan Murray, Audrey Hepburn—star of Gigi. An invitation was sent immediately to Walter Winchell at the Roney Plaza Hotel in Miami Beach, Florida, his winter headquarters, and it was stated therein that he was invited to this microphone to defend the statements made in his column about Miss Josephine Baker— defend himself with regard to the comments made about those paragraphs and the subsequent discussion by Josephine Baker and Ed Sullivan. That invitation is again issued herewith. The invitation is one that will remain standing at any time Walter Winchell or an accredited representative wish to appear here: they shall be welcome. And they may hear the recording and issue a statement of any kind.